AT THE TABLE OF

Jim Thompson

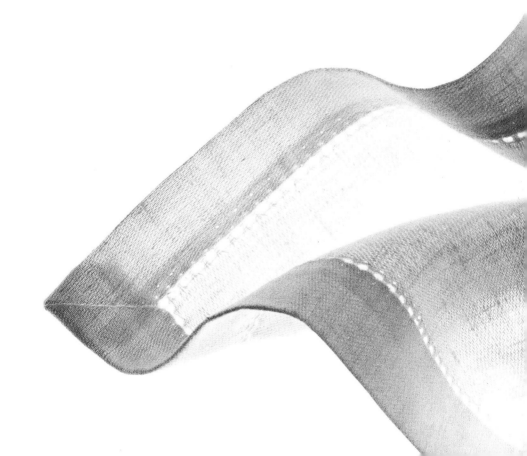

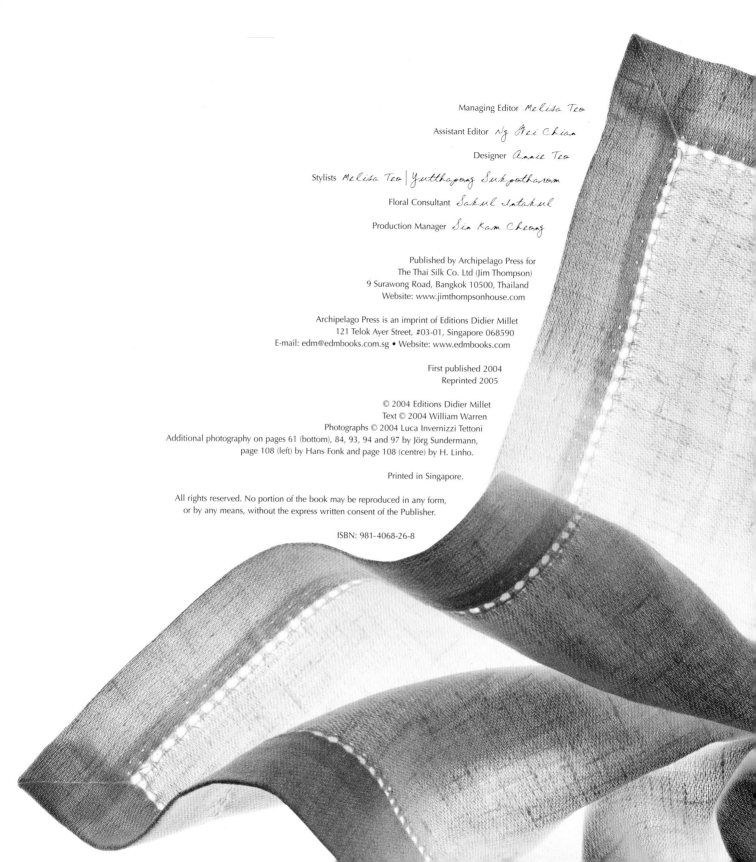

Managing Editor *Melisa Teo*

Assistant Editor *Ng Wei Chian*

Designer *Annie Teo*

Stylists *Melisa Teo* | *Yutthapong Sukpotharom*

Floral Consultant *Sakul Intakul*

Production Manager *Sin Kam Cheong*

Published by Archipelago Press for
The Thai Silk Co. Ltd (Jim Thompson)
9 Surawong Road, Bangkok 10500, Thailand
Website: www.jimthompsonhouse.com

Archipelago Press is an imprint of Editions Didier Millet
121 Telok Ayer Street, #03-01, Singapore 068590
E-mail: edm@edmbooks.com.sg • Website: www.edmbooks.com

First published 2004
Reprinted 2005

ISBN: 981-4068-26-8

AT THE TABLE OF

Jim Thompson

Introduction *William Warren*

Recipes *Chefs of the Jim Thompson restaurants*

Photography *Luca Invernizzi Tettoni*

ARCHIPELAGO PRESS

Contents

DINING WITH

Jim Thompson

LEFT: Bencharong, *a multi-colored ware with Thai designs that was made in China exclusively for export to Thailand.*

BELOW: *The seed pod of a lotus flower wrapped in Thai silk makes for an elegant place setting.*

RIGHT: *The dining table in the Jim Thompson house, set for one of the dinner parties that were such a central feature of his life there.*

The first time I was a guest at the table of Jim Thompson for dinner was on a warm, humid evening in March of 1959. The gathering was not held in the Thai-style residence that was soon to become so celebrated—that was still under construction, scheduled for completion the following month—but rather in a much smaller and more modest house he had built on Rama IV Road and that had been his Bangkok home for some six years.

It had a living room, dining room, and kitchen which were all on the ground floor, all unscreened with folding doors opening on the garden, while upstairs were two bedrooms and a bath equipped with a large water jar and a dipper. Even after all this time I can recall this layout clearly, for it was to become my home too, when I came to live in Bangkok little more than a year later.

No such future, however, could have seemed less likely to me on that first occasion. I had arrived in Bangkok

a few days before, ostensibly to write a script for a documentary film about Jim's revival of the Thai silk industry, though even then I had serious doubts that the project would ever be completed.

The film company I was working for was perilously close to collapse, my employer (back in America) was displaying signs of severe mental instability, and I harboured dark suspicions that the introduction he had furnished to Jim might not be received as warmly as he had assured me it would. (I was right about all these misgivings, for the company did collapse, the film never got made, and also I later found out that Jim loathed the man who had written the introduction for me).

But with characteristic hospitality, he received me warmly in his little silk shop, then located at the bottom of Surawong Road, and did much to make the weeks that I spent in Bangkok pleasant. He suggested a cheap hotel right across Lumpini Park from the Rama IV house, took me for lunch and a swim at the Royal Bangkok Sports Club, and at the end of the day also invited me for dinner with two girls who happened to be visiting at the time from New York.

On the night in question I walked across the park to his house, which I found with some difficulty. In those days, Rama IV Road was bordered by canals, lined with huge, umbrella-shaped rain trees, and poorly illuminated; only a narrow dirt driveway led to the wooden gates of his rather small compound.

Going out of the darkness and into the living room, though, was a revelation, as if one was entering a different world. Almost every inch of the walls and much of the floor space was filled with treasures, which made up part of the Asian art collection that Jim had been acquiring since he came to Thailand, and now more profusely

than usual since he was busily gathering new pieces to go into the Thai house. A jungle-like garden stretched right up to the tall open doorways on two sides, while through the third one could see the black water of a shallow canal glinting here and there, reflecting the moonlight filtering through the rain tree branches.

Such houses were becoming rare in Bangkok by the late '50s...but Jim had managed to acquire all or parts of six separate old structures...

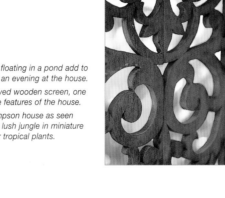

TOP RIGHT: Candles floating in a pond add to the atmosphere of an evening at the house.

RIGHT: Detail of carved wooden screen, one of many decorative features of the house.

LEFT: The Jim Thompson house as seen from the garden, a lush jungle in miniature of palms and other tropical plants.

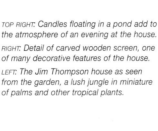

I was instantly enchanted, as were the other two guests. They were both young, pretty, and rich—typical, I would later learn, of one category of visitor (though by no means the only one) Jim often entertained. He liked having bright, attractive girls at his table, and if they happened to come from the wealthy East coast families he had grown up among, so much the better. (One of those that evening, who turned out to be a Standard Oil heiress, was so captivated by Bangkok and, in particular, by Jim's lifestyle that when she married she made her acceptance conditional on spending at least two years in the city; her husband, whose family Jim also knew, raised no objections.)

What did we eat on that evening? Here my memory fails, but I am fairly sure it was Thai, for Jim seldom served anything else at the time—what I remember from the meal was a clear soup, possibly with minced pork balls, then a spicy chicken or beef curry with rice, some sweet crispy noodles and stir-fried vegetables, finishing up with fresh mango and sticky rice (a delicacy which would have then been in season); all of which was prepared in a dingy kitchen I would come to know all

too well in the future. The truth was that neither the New York girls nor I paid that much attention to what we ate; we were too busy exclaiming over all the beautiful things that were scattered so casually around us in that rich little Aladdin's cave of wonders.

A few days before I left Bangkok, I had the good fortune to be one of the guests invited to a party for the official opening of Jim's Thai house. I had been there several times before during my stay, once when he took me on a tour of the Muslim weaving village across Klong Maha Nag where he bought much of his silk, on other occasions alone just to wander through it and watch with fascination as the carpenters added the finishing touches and the first plants were being installed in what was to be another lush garden.

ABOVE: A Chinese export ware teapot and bowl share space with an intricate Thai floral arrangement of jasmine blossoms.
RIGHT: The verdant grounds of the Thompson house created the perfect setting for his outdoor parties.
BELOW: Tantalizing snacks awaited guests who attended these lively gatherings.
OPPOSITE: Golden rays filtering through the foliage created an aura of calm.

Traditional Thai houses are usually rectangular in shape, though they come in different sizes, and the walls are pre-fabricated, hanging on a framework of stout columns so that they can easily be disassembled and moved to a new location. Such houses were becoming rare in Bangkok by the late '50s, as increasingly more Thais chose to live in Western-style homes, but Jim had managed to acquire all or parts of six separate old structures; another two were added some time later. Most were found upcountry, near the old capital of Ayutthaya, and were brought down the river stacked up on barges; but two, the future kitchen and the drawing room, came from the nearby weaving community and merely had to be carried across the *klong*.

In reassembling them, Jim was attempting something that had seldom, if ever, been done before. Normally each house would have stood as a separate unit, opening on to a common verandah, all raised several meters off the ground for a maximum of air circulation and to protect against floods

and wild animals; the stairway leading up would be outside the house and exposed to the elements. Jim, however, proposed to join the various rooms, so that one led to another without his having to go outside, replace the open verandah with a terrace overlooking the *klong* (on what was, architecturally, the front of the house), and enclose the stair to form a lofty entrance hall. Moreover, he wanted to have certain Western comforts such as indoor plumbing and bathrooms.

It was not quite so simple to execute, however, despite his pre-war training as an architect. A crew of skilled carpenters from Ayutthaya had to be brought to the site for the seven months which it took to build the main residence and also the three smaller outbuildings which were meant for the cook, gardener and houseboy, and even with all their expertise there were problems such as leaks at the points where the various steep, tiled roofs came together that took years to solve.

When I first saw it, the house was nearly finished. Three ceremonies had already been performed—one for raising the first column, one for siting the fanciful little abode of the spirit that would watch over the compound and had to be supplied with daily offerings, and one marking the official completion of the main house (though it was not actually to be ready for several more weeks)—all accompanied by elaborate rituals as decreed by Thai tradition.

Already, too, it was clearly going to be something out of the ordinary, a spectacular sight in Bangkok that had attracted a good deal of comment and many visitors during the construction period. Among them was the actress Anne Baxter, who had come with an introduction to Jim; he took her to see it and she was so overcome she insisted on coming back at night to view the elegant lines of the soaring roofs by moonlight from a boat in the *klong*.

It had been transformed by the evening of the housewarming party, however, and the effect was one of pure theater which few of those present would ever forget.

From the entrance hall, tiled with black-and-white marble Jim had salvaged from an old palace, we went up a majestic teak staircase, past high paneled walls hung with long, tapestry-like Thai paintings. In the upper rooms serene Thai Buddha images gazed down from antique gold-and-black lacquer cabinets, Khmer and Burmese

figures stood in niches that had been created from former windows, with Chinese porcelain bowls adorning the tables and cabinets, and many brilliant silk cushions scattered everywhere on chairs and couches.

Large crystal chandeliers hung from the ceilings of the splendid drawing room and the dining room, a Western touch (also from old palaces) that somehow blended perfectly with all the Asian art they illuminated. A classical Thai orchestra played during the meal on the seventeenth-century brick that covered the terrace outside, and after dinner there was also a performance by dancers in bejeweled costumes and ornate headdresses.

Jim had set up some tables in the breezy open area under the house, and had hired an outside caterer to prepare the food. Once again, my memory of what we ate is sketchy (a mixture of Thai and Chinese, I imagine, which was what people usually ordered for big dinners in those days) and once again for the same reason: I was duly caught up by the magical atmosphere, like the girls who had come to dinner a few weeks before. Then, I was already wondering how I could come back to Bangkok for good.

The effect was one of pure theater which few of those present would ever forget.

By the time I did, a year later, what people called Jim Thompson's Thai House was firmly established as a legend as powerful in its own way as his silk business. Indeed, so many strangers came wandering in to see it at all times that he had decided to open it two days a week to the public, with voluntary guides to show them around and the small entrance fee going to a local charity.

As noted above, I moved into the Rama IV house, sharing it with Charles Sheffield, Jim's assistant, and trying (without much success) to approximate the enchantment I had found on that first visit. I went to work at a local university and had no association with the silk company, but I frequently went with Charles to Jim's house for dinner or drinks, and so had an opportunity to see that fabled establishment at the peak of its glory.

Here one should say something about Bangkok in the '60s and the man himself, two things essential in any attempt to describe those evenings beside the *klong*. Then, as now, Bangkok was sprawling, contradictory, and more than slightly chaotic, but it was different

in many other ways from today's city. It was more traditional, for one thing, more Thai in the rhythms of its life if not in appearance. Waterways like Klong Maha Nag still played an important role in getting about, and noisy motor-boats were just beginning to shatter the tranquility along them.

Many of the amenities Westerners regarded as essential, such as hot water, telephones, air conditioning, gas stoves, even a reliable supply of electricity, were or still are a non-existent feature in most private houses. (Jim installed

an air conditioner in his study, which was mainly to protect his books, but did without all the other comforts, even when some of them became more accessible.)

There were no supermarkets and few good restaurants except in Chinatown. People entertained far more often at home, and shopping for fresh food meant a daily visit to the nearest market by the cook (happily, servants were plentiful), who prepared it on charcoal stoves in kitchens that horrified freshly-arrived expatriate housewives and

sent at least a few of them scurrying back to their native countries after a brief exposure to such intolerable living conditions.

Water was boiled before drinking and salad greens washed with an evil-looking violet-colored solution of potassium permanganate which was meant to kill any lurking germs. (Ice, however, which was almost certainly not made from boiled water, we bought by the block and consumed without any noticeable ill-effect. For a long time I was among those who genuinely believed that freezing killed all germs and was only enlightened by a mortified visitor who worked in tropical medicine and who had already consumed several chilled drinks. His conclusion on the matter was that we had somehow acquired some form of immunity despite our ignorance.)

The age of mass tourism had not yet arrived bringing its mixed blessings. Flying was expensive, and those who came by air were relatively few and mostly well-to-do. Others, generally Americans, arrived in large groups on cruise ships that scheduled their Asian voyages in the spring, to coincide with the cherry-blossom festival in Japan, which meant that they got to Bangkok during the worst of the hot season. Too large to come up the river, the ships anchored at its mouth and perspiring passengers were brought up in smaller boats for tours of the standard

LEFT: *An arrangement of radiant caladiums, anthurium leaves and ginger flowers.*

RIGHT: *An inviting daybed with brightly hued cushions on the terrace; the pavilion in the background leads to a landing stage on the canal that flows past the house.*

attractions like the Grand Palace and the Temple of the Emerald Buddha and, if they were lucky, an hour or so in Jim Thompson's little silk shop, which was air-conditioned (at least downstairs) and thus a welcome relief, as well as full of alluring things to buy.

Things were gradually beginning to change, especially toward the end of the decade as the war in Vietnam accelerated and increasing amounts of foreign aid poured in; but for most of those years Bangkok was still essentially the same city that had so beguiled Jim

when he first settled down there in the late '40s, and that I suspect he secretly hoped would always remain that way.

He himself was a much more complicated person than many realized. He came from a comfortably wealthy background, and surrounded himself in his new home with a trove of rare and beautiful objects; yet amid all those splendors he lived a simple, even spartan life. All his meals were still cooked over charcoal, just as they had been in his first house, he slept without air conditioning, and the great drawing

room remained open to dogs, cats, bantam chickens and assorted pets, as well as swarms of hungry mosquitoes after dark. He got up early and worked hard all day, often joining the sales staff in the shop where his obvious enthusiasm for his product worked with even the most difficult customers who visited his shop.

(House guests were not always happy about sharing the inconveniences he took for granted, however. After frequent complaints about the short, rock-hard bed in the guest room, the sweltering heat, and the necessity of clearing out when the house was opened to tourists, Jim finally added an air-conditioned wing on one side and kept it off-limits to casual visitors.)

He would willingly spend large sums to acquire new pieces of art for his collection, but in other respects he was notably frugal. Though guests might dine off Ming blue-and-white porcelain plates, they drank cocktails and wine from the cheapest available glassware, and the same attitude extended to the food he served.

If a visiting friend donated some imported luxury like smoked salmon, caviar, or *pâté de foie gras*, it would be generously shared at the table, but

otherwise everything came from the local fresh food market and tended to be the sort of basic fare that could be found on the most ordinary Thai table.

Charles Sheffield remembered Jim saying once that he could feed six people well for 100 baht, which even in those days would have meant stretching it awfully far. (He may have actually tried it on a couple of occasions, however. I remember a dish that consisted of a head of baked cauliflower sprinkled with seasoned bread crumbs. A stranger might help himself to a generous portion of this, assuming that a second head would in due course appear; those of us who had seen it before would be much more careful, for we knew there was only one and when it was finished, that was that.)

Not being such a fan of Thai food that I was willing to eat it at every

meal, I had brought with me from America a book of Charleston recipes, the ingredients for quite a few of which could be found readily in Bangkok. I then proceeded to try these out with my cook, making substitutions when necessary; and if they worked, she would translate the results into Thai for future reference. Jim heard about this and borrowed the translations: soon exotic new dishes such as Chicken Country Captain, Deviled Crab and Tomato Aspic began to appear at his dinners, though he always complained about the exorbitant cost of such "fancy food".

While he entertained the rich and famous, he was equally hospitable to visitors who had little to recommend them, but who could make amusing conversation or had expertise in a field that interested him, like Chinese export porcelain or early Thai culture. His permanent circle of local friends was

TOP RIGHT: Thai hors d'œuvres *served on the petals of a banana flower.*

LEFT: Lighted candles give off a warm glow.

OPPOSITE: Pink ginger flowers sitting in glasses along the top of the parapet on the terrace.

While he entertained the rich and famous, he was equally hospitable to visitors who had little to recommend them...

small, not many more than a dozen in all, and he often called on them to help out with answering questions about the house and its contents when there was a large crowd of outsiders, which increasingly became the case as plane fares dropped and Bangkok became a standard stop on the tourist route.

Jim had been an institution for at least ten years when I met him, ever since Irene Sharaff had made Thai silk famous the world over with her gorgeous costumes for the original Broadway production of *The King and I*. He was being written about in *Life*, *Reader's Digest*, the *New York Times*, and dozens of other publications.

His silk was being used by leading fashion designers and interior decorators. Nearly everyone who came to Bangkok, whether dignitaries or tourists, stopped at his shop, and many of them brought letters of introduction. Since he invited most of these to come for dinner or drinks, he had become well-known as a host long before he built the house that was the ideal setting for his entertaining.

Some of the early visitors were friends or acquaintances from his pre-war days, like the Woolworth heiress Barbara Hutton, who was so entranced with his silk that she used it extensively

RIGHT: *Raw silk threads are woven into fine drapes that embellish the living room.*
BELOW: *Thai silk carpets in a panoply of vibrant colors.*
OPPOSITE: *Jim Thompson's silks are characterized by their finesse and quality of design.*

in both her Moroccan and Mexican houses (and ordered new supplies woven for redecoration almost every year).

Others were the kind of people who always seemed to have an introduction to the leading social figures wherever they went, no matter how remote; thus the house saw a procession of figures such as photographer Cecil Beaton and writer Truman Capote, both of whom turned up in the late '50s, as did the critic Ward Morehouse and the

theatrical director Joshua Logan (both of whom were introduced by Gertrude Lawrence, who had created the role of Anna in *The King and I*), the powerful newspaper columnist Joseph Alsop, author James Michener and Senator William Fulbright, whose scholarships were sending countless Thais to America for their education.

Then there was a considerably larger group who had distinguished themselves by buying a great deal of

silk in the shop, or simply by being attractive in some way that appealed to Jim. Early on, when his business was still struggling to gain wider repute, he regarded such entertaining as a significant part of the process (which it probably was: a way of increasing sales or at least generating publicity); and by then it was no longer really necessary as it had become as much a feature of his regular routine as the daily trips to his weavers and the hours spent in his shop.

The truth was that no matter how hard he worked during the day, Jim was a naturally gregarious man and liked having people around in the evening. The only solitary pleasure he enjoyed, as far as I knew, was listening to recordings of classical music, and one of the few personal luxuries he allowed himself was an excellent stereo set; otherwise, it was a rare evening when at least a few guests were not seated around his table, sometimes invited at the last minute.

William Klausner, now President of The James H. W. Thompson Foundation, remembers being invited when he was an obscure young graduate student on his way to live for a year in a northeastern village. "Jim not only had me to dinner," he says, "but invited some

other people he thought I would enjoy meeting and even arranged for some musicians to play northeastern music."

The Thai house, of course, provided a much grander background for such gatherings, and he took full advantage of it. This large establishment was run by a surprisingly small but competent staff. There was a Chinese cook, a Thai maid, a gardener and an efficient, imperturbable houseboy named Yee.

All of them had been with Jim since the Rama IV days, and all were expert at adjusting to his sometimes unpredictable ways, even though their English was limited and Jim on his part never learned more than a few words of Thai. A message sent from the office at the last minute saying there would be eight rather than four for dinner, or sixteen for an impromptu cocktail party, aroused no great consternation, and there was seldom any sign of hasty preparations or disorganization.

Dinner was rarely for more than eight or ten, for that was the most that the antique dining tables (which had once been used for gaming in the Grand Palace) could accommodate. There would be a flower arrangement in the middle, sometimes a traditional Thai one composed of bachelor's buttons (*Gomphrene globosa*) or fragrant jasmine buds set tightly together in a conical shape such that they closely resembled a piece of complex porcelain, sometimes an informal mass of orchid sprays, gardenias and other ornamental blooms gathered from the garden or bought in the market. (Yee was responsible for this, as well as for others elsewhere in the house.)

Thai silk place mats and napkins matched Chinese blue-and-white export dishes and bronzeware cutlery, gleaming in the flattering light of the chandelier. A set of Thai paintings on cloth adorned one wall, while elsewhere cabinets displayed more of the porcelain that Jim started collecting in earnest shortly after moving into the house.

An extraordinary assortment of guests gathered in this memorable setting almost every night during the eight years he lived in his house by the *klong*. One of the earliest, in 1960, was W. Somerset Maugham, who was on a farewell trip to Asia, where so many of his stories had been set, and who celebrated his 86th birthday while in Bangkok; in a thank-you note to Jim, he observed, "You have not only beautiful things but what is rare you have arranged them with faultless taste."

LEFT: A traditional Thai arrangement in a bencharong bowl; the flowers are embedded in shaped mounds of damp sand or sawdust.

BELOW: Thai silk napkins in a blue-and-white print complement the patterns on Chinese export ware used at dinner parties.

OPPOSITE: Heliconia blossoms adorn a carved antique altar table in the dining room.

The truth was that no matter how hard he worked during the day, Jim was a naturally gregarious man and liked having people around in the evening.

The clarion-voiced Broadway star Ethel Merman came with her husband of the time, airline president Robert Six, and woke the residents of the weaving village when she serenaded Jim's pet cockatoo to the tune of *Hello Dolly*.

Doris Duke, known as "the richest girl in the world", showed up with a bodyguard whose gun kept slipping alarmingly out of his jacket and developed such an enthusiasm for what she saw that she immediately began buying old Thai houses and art with the idea of putting up a "Thai village" on her estate in Hawaii. (This scheme was unfortunately never realized; crates of house components and objects were still unpacked when she died 40 years later, and were finally being catalogued by her estate in 2003.)

A steady stream of journalists, editors and publishers were invited, among them Henry Luce of *Time* and *Life*, and, with the war in Vietnam, an

increasing number of high-ranking military figures, largely due to General Edwin Black, an old friend from Jim's army days, who became a regular visitor and house guest when he was appointed commander of the U.S. Support Forces in Thailand.

Always, too, there were the lively young visitors Jim enjoyed having around him, the scholars eager to see his art collection and talk to him about it, fashion designers like Pierre Balmain who made clothes for the Queen of Thailand, members of the local French community with whom Jim could chat in their language (which he had learned from a governess as a child), diplomats like the American, British and French ambassadors, prominent Thais he had known socially and professionally since his earliest years, and the inevitable wealthy tourists whose only apparent claim to distinction was that they spent a large amount of money in the shop.

They were fascinated by the story of how Jim had ended up in such an exotic place, and how he had taken a traditional craft and given it extraordinary new life. It was a good story, almost unique in the Asia of those days, and he was always willing

*"You have not only beautiful things but what is rare you have arranged them with faultless taste."
(W. Somerset Maugham)*

ABOVE: Western table settings combine with distinctively Thai architecture.

LEFT: Drinks were always a prelude to an evening of conversation and fine food.

OPPOSITE: Modern dining décor contrasts with the softly-lit teak walls of the house.

to repeat it with as much enthusiasm as if he were telling it for the first time, with some embellishment. (He might, for instance, tell a wide-eyed group of ladies that Thai silk acquired its distinctive lustre from being washed in the murky waters of the *klong*, an assertion that seemed less improbable when they cast their eyes across the terrace and saw lengths of richly colored fabric drying on railings outside weavers' houses.)

They were equally curious about his house and collection, and here it was always found that he had an endless supply of still more interesting lore—he was able to tell eager listeners about how that ornately decorated wall leading off the drawing room had once been the front of a Chinese pawn shop, why it was considered unlucky to step on the slightly raised thresholds of the doors, what sort of subjects that were depicted in the Thai paintings on almost

LEFT: *Stairway leading down into the garden from the guest wing, added to the house several years after it was built.*

BELOW: *A quaint marble-topped table in the area beneath the main house.*

RIGHT: *An annexe in the garden, built to display a collection of nineteenth-century paintings depicting daily Thai life.*

every wall and the reasons for their peculiar style, when that haunting Buddha image in the study had been carved, and countless others.

In the last four or five years, an important part of the scene was Cocky, Jim's beloved white cockatoo. The handsome bird with a bright yellow crest seemed to enjoy being a focus of attention and attended nearly every dinner and cocktail party, perched either on a chair or Jim's shoulder and responding eagerly to music played on the stereo system. (A bright red and blue lorikeet proved less popular with guests; it had a nasty habit of biting people, sometimes drawing blood.)

Sadly, few of these people are still around to share their memories of what it was like to spend an evening with Jim Thompson. Those who survive, however, almost unanimously agree that it was a singular experience, one that combined good company with a setting of beauty and richness to create a blend that would be exceptional anywhere.

In preparing this introduction I asked one of the former guests, a woman of taste and sophistication, what she could recall of the food served on such occasions. "I remember it as being delicious," she replied, "but I couldn't for the life of me tell you what it was. Anything would have been delicious in those surroundings. It wasn't just the food, you see, or even just the people you met there or the lovely things everywhere you looked. It was the whole atmosphere. I've never experienced anything like it."

Anne Tofield, who lived in Bangkok and worked in the silk shop in the mid-'60s, also agrees that it was an exceptional experience, commenting that "part of the magic was the feeling it would all disappear in the morning... and I think a lot of it did."

She remembers an evening when Senator Edward Kennedy, his wife Joan, and a group of "hangers-on" were also present: "Joan K. was enthralled with the house and kept calling to Ted to come and see various things. He wouldn't leave his cronies to join her and in desperation she said, loudly, 'He is in the most beautiful house in the world and doesn't know where he is!' It was a sad moment because it was true."

The last time I ever had dinner with Jim was in the spring of 1967, several days before he was leaving for a holiday in the Cameron Highlands of Malaysia.

It was unusual in that Charles and I were the only guests, for it was supposed to be a working session, one that had already been put off several times. I was doing the text for a picture book on the house and collection, with photographs by a gifted New Zealander named Brian Brake, and lacked sufficient information about several objects; the manuscript

...it was a singular experience, one that combined good company with a setting of memorable beauty and richness to create a blend that would be exceptional anywhere.

RIGHT: Classic Thai food was always a feature of Jim Thompson's parties.

BELOW: The Jim Thompson restaurant is housed in a traditional Thai structure in a compound adjoining that of the main residence.

OPPOSITE: The terrace and drawing room at night, when the magical allure of the house was at its most potent.

was already behind schedule and had to be sent off to the publishers in Japan. It was the sort of niggling but necessary chore Jim disliked, and he was still tired from the stress of opening a new, larger shop just a week earlier. He did it with good humor, however, and we finished at a comparatively early hour.

He saw us off in the courtyard, Cocky sitting on his shoulder and a favorite dog by his side—a typical end to an evening at the house. Neither Charles nor I had any sense of

foreboding, any idea that we would never see him standing there again.

In the weeks that followed, first with the stunning news that he had failed to return from a supposed walk while staying at Moonlight Cottage, a holiday home owned by friends, on Easter Sunday afternoon, and then with the frustrations of a long search that ultimately proved futile, there was an air of unreality about the strangely silent house. Yee continued to arrange flowers and the other servants went about their

chores, just as though Jim would be coming back any moment; indeed, they were convinced he would and did not abandon hope for a very long time.

There were a few social gatherings at the house during that gloomy time, most of them when Jim's brother Henry and his sister Elinor arrived to deal with various necessary matters.

The one I remember best was given several months after he disappeared by an old friend named Elizabeth Lyons, an Asian art expert with the Philadelphia Museum, who had often stayed there before as a guest.

Feeling that the staff needed a bit of cheer, she arranged a small dinner, with the table set up on the terrace. There were about seven of us, as I remember, all of whom had been residents and frequent guests in the past, and the house was lit up in all its customary splendor. Only one, a French woman who worked in the shop, declined to come, saying that she felt the emotional strain would be too great.

Perhaps she was right. As hard as we all tried to pretend and have a good time, the essential catalyst was missing; even Cocky knew it and sat sullenly on the back of his chair,

LEFT: *Deftly folded lotus buds, often seen in Thai decorations, enhance luxurious silk-wrapped chairs.*

RIGHT: *The geometric tiles of the entrance hall form a striking background for silk cushions with contemporary designs.*

refusing to play his usual role of entertainer. It was a muted evening; memories were still too fresh to recapture the spirit that had enlivened so many others around that table.

Jim would hardly recognize his beloved Bangkok today, and I doubt he would like many of its changes. I feel sure, though, that he would be proud of the fact that his house remains substantially as he last saw it, with his collection intact, that it still attracts admiring visitors, and that it has even acquired new facilities where they can relax and savor an atmosphere now almost unique in the surrounding city.

If guests can no longer actually dine at the table of Jim Thompson, they can still do so at three restaurants bearing his name. One is in a Thai-style building just outside the gates of his compound, while the others are in the main silk shop and in an old house on Saladaeng Road. Some of the dishes served at these establishments are described in the pages that follow.

Starters

From the delicate crunch of a betel leaf to the savory crackle of a spring roll, the versatility and variety of Thai starters make them the ideal companion for a glass of chilled beer.

▷ Betel-Leaf Snacks (Miang Kham)

WRAPPING LEAVES ▷ Betel or lettuce leaves

FILLING ▷ ¾ cup (60 g/2 oz) grated coconut, oven-toasted until light brown
2 small limes, unpeeled and diced • 4 to 5 fresh bird's eye chilies, finely sliced
6 tbsp diced shallots • 6 tbsp roasted peanuts • 6 tbsp small dried shrimp

SAUCE ▷ ¾ cup (60 g/2 oz) shallots, coarsely sliced
¾ cup (60 g/2 oz) fresh galangal, slivered and roasted until fragrant
1 tbsp shrimp paste, roasted until fragrant • 1½ tsp sliced ginger
¼ cup (20 g/⅔ oz) grated coconut, oven-toasted until light brown
1½ cups (115 g/4 oz) small dried shrimp • 1¾ cups (420 ml/14¼ fl oz) water
1¼ cups (230 g/8⅛ oz) palm sugar, broken into small chunks • 2 tbsp sugar
salt to taste

To prepare the sauce, pound the shallots and galangal finely with a mortar
and pestle. Add the shrimp paste, ginger, coconut and dried shrimp, and
pound until smooth. Add this mixture with the water and both types of
sugar to a pot. Bring this to a boil over medium heat and simmer on low
heat until reduced to about 1 cup (250 ml/8½ fl oz). Add salt to taste.
Remove from heat and transfer the sauce to a small bowl.
To serve, separate the filling ingredients into individual bowls. Place a
small amount of each ingredient in the center of a wrapping leaf, top with
a spoonful of sauce and fold into a parcel.

Serves 1 to 2

◁ Heavenly Beef (Neua Sawarn)

4 coriander roots, chopped • ¼ tsp salt • 3 tbsp chopped garlic
2 tsp white peppercorns • 10½ oz (300 g) beef sirloin, sliced ¼-in (0.75-cm) thick,
2½-in (6-cm) long • 2 tsp sugar • 2 tbsp oyster sauce • 1½ tbsp light soy sauce
1 tsp coriander seeds, lightly crushed • oil for deep-frying
1 cup (250 ml/8½ fl oz) chili sauce

Pound the coriander root, salt, garlic and peppercorns into a fine paste with a
mortar and pestle. Work this paste, along with the sugar, oyster sauce and
light soy sauce, into the beef slices and leave to marinate for 4 hours.
Remove the beef from the marinade, rub in the crushed coriander seeds and
leave to dry in a warm place for approximately 20 hours. Deep-fry the beef in
medium to hot oil until well done. Serve with chili sauce.

Serves 1 to 2

▷ Sweet Chili Sauce (Nahm Jim Gai Waan)

4 tbsp chopped fresh red chilies • 1¼ cups (190 g/6¾ oz) garlic, chopped
5 cups (1 kg/2 lbs 3 oz) sugar • ¼ cup (115 g/17 oz) salt
1¼ cups (300 ml/10⅛ fl oz) vinegar • 1 cup (250 ml/8½ oz) water

Pound the chilies and garlic together finely with a mortar and pestle. Boil the
sugar, salt and vinegar with the water in a pot. Mix well and add the chili-and-
garlic paste. Simmer until thick and remove from heat. Allow to cool and serve.

Makes 4 cups (1 L/1 qt ½ fl oz)

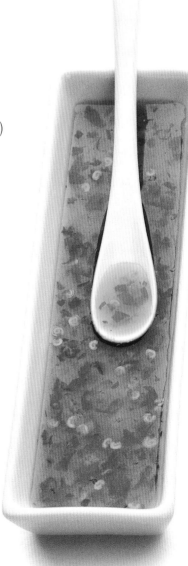

◁ Fried Chicken Wings (Peak Gai Tod)

2 coriander roots • 3 cloves garlic, chopped • ½ tsp ground white pepper
2 tsp light soy sauce • 2 tsp oyster sauce • ½ tsp garlic powder
4 chicken wings, cut at the first joint • oil for deep-frying
1 cup (250 ml/8½ fl oz) sweet chili sauce (see recipe above)

Pound the coriander roots and garlic into a fine paste with a mortar and pestle.
Add the white pepper, light soy sauce, oyster sauce and garlic powder, then
mix well. Marinate the chicken wings in the mixture overnight. Deep-fry the
wings in medium to hot oil for 7 to 10 minutes or until golden brown. Serve
with sweet chili sauce.

Serves 1 to 2

▽ Shrimp in Crispy Blankets (Gung Hom Pha)

2 coriander roots • 1 clove garlic, peeled
6 whole white peppercorns, crushed
½ tsp salt • 1 tsp light soy sauce
1 tsp oyster sauce
8 large shrimp, shelled and deveined with tails intact
8 small spring-roll wrappers • oil for deep-frying
1 cup (250 ml/8½ fl oz) plum sauce (see Basics)

Pound the coriander roots, garlic, white peppercorns and salt finely with a mortar and pestle. Season the mixture with light soy sauce and oyster sauce. Marinate the shrimp in this mixture for 15 to 20 minutes before rolling each shrimp in a spring-roll wrapper, covering the body and leaving the tail exposed. Deep-fry in medium to hot oil until golden brown. Serve with plum sauce.

Serves 1 to 2

▽ Shrimp Cakes (Tod Man Gung)

4 coriander roots, scraped and chopped • 6 cloves garlic
¼ tsp chopped ginger • pinch of ground white pepper • pinch of salt
10½ oz (300 g) uncooked minced shrimp • pinch of white sugar
1 tbsp light soy sauce • 1 cup (115 g/4 oz) breadcrumbs • oil for deep-frying
1 cup (250 ml/8½ fl oz) plum sauce (see Basics)

Pound the coriander roots, garlic, ginger, pepper and salt into a fine paste with a mortar and pestle. Combine this with the shrimp until firm and sticky. Season with sugar and soy sauce. Roll this mixture into 1-in (2.5-cm) balls before flattening into cakes. Coat evenly with bread-crumbs and deep-fry in oil until golden brown. Serve with plum sauce.

Serves 1 to 2

▽ Deep-Fried Chicken Spring Rolls (Poh Pia Gai)

⅜ cup (20 g/½ oz) vermicelli • 1 tbsp oil • 1 clove garlic, chopped
2 coriander roots, finely chopped • ⅓ cup (50 g/1¾ oz) minced chicken
⅔ cup (20 g/¾ oz) shiitake mushrooms, chopped
⅛ cup (10 g/¼ oz) carrot, peeled and grated
¼ cup (20 g/½ oz) chopped spring onion • 2 tsp soy sauce • 1 tsp oyster sauce
pinch of sugar • 1 tsp cornflour • 1 tbsp water • 8 spring roll wrappers
oil for deep-frying • 1 cup (250 ml/8½ fl oz) plum sauce (see Basics)

To prepare the filling, break the vermicelli into 2-in (5-cm) pieces. Cover with boiling water and soak for 3 to 4 minutes or until soft. Drain and set aside. Heat the oil in a frying pan or wok, and stir-fry the garlic and coriander roots for about 1 minute. Add the minced chicken and fry for another 3 to 4 minutes, stirring the mixture to prevent clumping. Add the mushrooms, carrot, spring onion, soy sauce, oyster sauce, sugar and vermicelli. Stir well and set aside to cool. In a small bowl, work the cornflour and water into a paste. Place 1 spring-roll wrapper on a flat surface with a corner towards you. Moisten the edges with the cornflour paste. Place 1 tbsp of filling in the center, spreading it out into a cylinder. Fold the nearest corner over the mixture and roll towards the center. Fold in the left and right corners to the middle and continue rolling to the top. Seal the edges with cornflour paste. Repeat this process with the remaining wrappers and filling. Deep-fry the rolls in medium to hot oil until golden brown. Serve with plum sauce.

Serves 1 to 2

◁ Pork Balls in Golden Threads

(Muu Sarong)

⅝ cup (1¾ oz/50 g) egg noodles
2 cups (260 g/9⅛ oz) minced pork
1 tbsp minced coriander root • 1 tbsp minced garlic
½ tbsp minced ginger • ½ tbsp lemon grass
½ tsp ground white pepper • 1 tbsp oyster sauce
1 tbsp curry paste • 2 tbsp wheat flour • 1 egg
pinch of salt • pinch of sugar • oil for deep-frying

Cook the egg noodles in boiling water for 4 to 5 minutes. Strain and leave to soak in cold water for 2 minutes, then drain noodles and set aside. Combine the minced pork and all the other ingredients in a large bowl. Knead the pork mixture until firm and roll into ½-in (1.25 cm) balls. Wrap each pork ball with 3 strands of the cooked noodles and deep-fry in hot oil until noodles are golden brown.

Serves 1 to 2

Salads

▷ Fried Fish Maw
& Cashew Nut Salad (Yam Sarm Krob)

⅓ cup (30 g/1 oz) dried fish maw • ⅓ cup (30 g/1 oz) dried squid
oil for frying • ¼ cup (20 g/¾ oz) fried cashew nuts, chopped
½ cup (20 g/¾ oz) finely sliced spring onion
⅜ cup (30 g/1 oz) finely sliced shallots
⅛ cup (10 g/⅜ oz) chopped mint leaves and coriander

DRESSING ▷ 3 fresh red chilies, crushed • 2 tbsp freshly squeezed lime juice
2 tbsp fish sauce • 1 tbsp sugar • 1 tsp roasted chili paste (see Basics)

To prepare the dressing, put the lime juice, fish sauce, sugar, chili paste and red
chilies in a bowl. Mix and set aside. Cut the fish maw into 3-in (7.5-cm) pieces and
fry in medium to hot oil. Drain and set aside. Fry the dried squid in medium to hot
oil. Set aside to cool, then cut into 1-in (2.5-cm) pieces. Mix the fish maw, squid
and cashew nuts with the dressing. Add the spring onions and shallots, mix well
and garnish with mint and coriander leaves.

Serves 1 to 2

*Color and texture are important considerations in Thai salads,
and the three classic taste notes of spiciness, sourness and saltiness
are a perennial feature.*

▷ Spicy Shrimp Salad with Lemon Grass (Yam Ta Krai)

⅜ cup (30 g/1 oz) dried squid, chopped • 3 large shrimp, shelled and deveined
oil for frying • ⅜ oz (10 g) chopped spring onion

DRESSING ▷ ⅝ cup (50 g/1¾ oz) finely chopped lemon grass
8 bird's eye chilies, chopped • ¼ cup (20 g/¾ oz) chopped shallots
2½ tsp sugar • 2 tbsp lime juice • 2 tbsp fish sauce
1 tsp roasted chili paste (see Basics) • 2 tbsp stock

To prepare the dressing, combine the lemon grass, chilies, shallots, sugar,
lime juice, fish sauce, chili paste and stock in a bowl and mix well. Set
aside. Deep-fry the dried squid and shrimp separately until golden brown
and cooked, then toss with the dressing. Garnish with chopped spring onion.

Serves 1 to 2

▷ Squid Salad (Yam Pla Meuk)

4¼ oz (120 g) squid, cleaned and scored
¼ cup (20 g/¾ oz) onion, finely sliced
2 small tomatoes, cut into wedges
3 stalks Thai celery, chopped
3 stalks spring onion, finely sliced
handful of mint and coriander leaves, chopped

DRESSING ▷ 6 fresh bird's eye chilies, crushed
2 cloves garlic, chopped • pinch of salt
2 tbsp lime juice • 2 tsp sugar • 2 tbsp fish sauce

To prepare the dressing, pound the chilies, garlic and salt into
a fine paste with a mortar and pestle. Add the lime juice,
sugar and fish sauce. Stir and set aside. Clean the squid and
cut the body and tentacles into 1½-in (3.75-cm) pieces. Blanch
the squid quickly in boiling salted water. Combine the squid with the
onions, tomatoes, celery and spring onions. Dress and garnish with
chopped mint and coriander leaves.

Serves 1 to 2

▷ Spicy Deep-Fried Catfish Salad
(Yam Pla Duk Fuu)

1 (400 g/14 1/8 oz) smoked catfish • oil for deep-frying • 10 bird's eye chilies, chopped
1/2 tbsp grated palm sugar • 2 tbsp lime juice • 1/2 tbsp fish sauce • 3 large shallots, thinly sliced
1/4 cup (60 g/2 1/8 oz) green mango, shredded • 2 tbsp roasted peanuts

Remove the skin and bones from the catfish. Break the flesh into flakes with a fork. Heat the oil in a
wok to medium-high heat. Place half of the catfish flesh into the hot oil and fry until golden-brown
and crispy on both sides. Fry the rest of the fish in the same manner. Set aside to cool.
To prepare the dressing, mix the chilies, sugar, lime juice and fish sauce together. Add the shallots
and shredded mango. Toss the catfish and dressing together with the roasted peanuts. Serve on a
bed of lettuce.

Serves 1 to 2

▷ Spicy Minced Chicken Salad

(Larb Gai)

¾ cup (100 g/3½ oz) skinless chicken breast, minced
1 clove garlic, chopped • ¼ tsp salt
3 tbsp chicken stock (see Basics) • ¼ tsp white sugar
1 tbsp lime juice • 1 tsp roasted chili powder • 1 tbsp fish sauce
1 tbsp sliced shallots • 1 tbsp shredded long-leaf coriander
handful of mint and coriander leaves, chopped
1 tbsp ground roasted rice (see Basics)

Mix the minced chicken with the garlic and salt. Heat the stock in a wok or
saucepan and season with the sugar and a little lime juice. Add the chicken mixture and
simmer for 3 minutes or until the chicken is slightly cooked. Stir in the remaining lime juice,
chili powder and fish sauce, followed by the shallots, chopped mint and coriander leaves. Toss well.
Garnish with shredded long-leaf coriander and ground roasted rice.

Serves 1 to 2

◁ Thai Beef Salad

(Pla Neua)

5¼ oz (150 g) sirloin steak
3 shallots, thinly sliced
2 large cloves garlic, thinly sliced
2 kaffir lime leaves, finely shredded
1 long red chili, sliced • 12 sprigs fresh mint
1 small cucumber, peeled, deseeded and thinly sliced

DRESSING ▷ 2 stalks lemon grass, white sections thinly sliced
10 bird's eye chilies, finely chopped • 2 tsp white sugar • 2 tbsp lime juice
2½ tbsp fish sauce • 2 tsp roasted chili paste (see Basics)

To prepare the dressing, combine the dressing ingredients in a bowl. Mix well and set aside. Chargrill the beef until medium-rare and set aside for 10 minutes. Slice into 1-by-3-in (2.5-by-7.5-cm) pieces and combine with the shallots, garlic, lime leaves, chilies, mint and cucumber. Toss well. Dress the salad and serve on a bed of lettuce.

Serves 1 to 2

▽ Spicy Papaya Salad (Som Tam)

3 cloves garlic, chopped • 5 green bird's eye chilies
1 tbsp dried shrimp • 1 tbsp roasted peanuts • 1½ tsp grated palm sugar
1½ tbsp fish sauce • 1½ tbsp lime juice • 2 cherry tomatoes, quartered
½ cup (75 g/2⅝ oz) snake beans, cut into 1-in (2.5-cm) sections
2½ cups (200 g/7 oz) green papaya, peeled and grated into thin strips
2 cooked shrimp, peeled and deveined

Pound the garlic and chilies roughly with a mortar and pestle. Add the dried shrimp and peanuts and pound into a coarse paste. Stir in the palm sugar, fish sauce and lime juice. Mix in the cherry tomatoes and string beans and continue pounding lightly. Transfer this mixture to a large bowl, then add the green papaya and bruise with the pestle. Toss well and garnish with the cooked shrimp. Serve with wedges of cabbage.

Serves 1 to 2

▽ Pomelo Salad (Yam Som Oo)

1 tbsp thinly sliced garlic • 1 tbsp thinly sliced shallots
2 tbsp grated coconut, roasted • 1 cup (150 g/5½ oz) pomelo segments
2 to 3 cooked shrimp, peeled and deveined • 1 tsp chopped red chilies
1 tbsp ground roasted peanuts • 2 tbsp coriander leaves

DRESSING ▷ ½ cup (125 ml/4¼ fl oz) coconut milk • 2 tsp grated palm sugar
1 tbsp fish sauce • 2 tbsp lime juice • 2 tsp roasted chili paste (see Basics)

To prepare the dressing, boil the coconut milk, palm sugar, fish sauce,
chili paste and lime juice in a wok for 10 minutes. Set aside to cool.
Stir-fry the garlic and shallots separately for 1 minute, then combine them
in a bowl. Add the roasted coconut, pomelo, shrimp, chilies and ground
roasted peanuts. Dress the salad and garnish with coriander leaves.

Serves 1 to 2

△ Deep-Fried Morning Glory Salad (Yam Pak Bung Grob)

7 oz (200 g) morning glory, cleaned and trimmed • oil for deep-frying

BATTER ▷ ½ cup (57.5 g/4½ oz) wheat flour • pinch of salt • pinch of pepper
½ cup (57.5 g/4½ oz) tempura flour • 2 cups (500 ml/1 pt 1 fl oz) water
1 tbsp oil

Trim and clean the morning glory in cold water. Pat dry and set aside.
To prepare the batter, mix all the batter ingredients in a bowl.
Coat each bundle of morning glory with batter, shaking off any excess.
Deep-fry in oil until golden brown. Serve with spicy sauce.

Serves 1 to 2

△ Spicy Sauce

(Nahm Yam)

3 cloves garlic, chopped
5 bird's eye chilies, chopped
1 coriander root, scraped and chopped
3 tbsp lime juice • 1 tbsp pickled garlic juice
2 tbsp fish sauce • 1 tsp melted palm sugar
⅜ cup (50 g/3½ oz) minced pork, cooked
2 cooked shrimp, shelled and deveined

Combine all the ingredients in a bowl and mix
well before serving.

Makes 1 cup (250 ml/8½ fl oz)

▽ Grilled Pork Salad

(Nahm Dtok Muu)

5¼ oz (150 g) pork tenderloin • oil for grilling or pan-frying
4 red shallots, sliced • handful of mint and coriander leaves, chopped
1 tbsp chopped spring onion • 1 tbsp chopped coriander
1 tbsp ground roasted rice (see Basics)

DRESSING ▷ 3 to 4 dried red bird's eye chilies, fried • 1 tsp roasted chili powder
2 tsp white sugar • 1½ tbsp lime juice • 2½ tbsp fish sauce

To prepare the dressing, mix all the dressing ingredients in a bowl
and set aside. Grill or pan-fry the pork to your taste. Set aside for 5
minutes. Slice the pork and combine with the shallots and herbs. Dress
the salad and garnish with chopped coriander and ground roasted rice.

Serves 1 to 2

Soups | Curries

Thai soups, ranging from light broths which cleanse the palate to thick concoctions dense in ingredient and flavor, serve as a complement to the meal. Curries differ in taste, color and texture from region to region. Indian and Muslim influences dictate the generous use of dried spices found in northern and southern Thai curries.

▽ Spicy Beef Curry (Gaeng Panaeng Neua)

5¼ oz (150 g) beef sirloin cubes • 1½ cups (375 ml/12⅝ fl oz) coconut milk
1 cup (250 ml/8½ fl oz) coconut cream • 1 tbsp panaeng curry paste (see Basics) • pinch of salt
2 tbsp grated palm sugar • 1 tbsp fish sauce • 1 long red chili, deseeded and sliced lengthwise
handful of Thai basil leaves • 1 kaffir lime leaf, torn

Blanch the beef to soften it, then rinse and set aside. In a hot wok, bring the coconut milk to a boil, add the beef, then braise over low to medium heat for 2 hours. In a separate pot or wok, simmer the coconut cream over medium heat for 5 minutes. Increase the heat and add the red curry paste, frying for another 10 minutes. Season with salt, palm sugar and fish sauce. Reduce the heat and add the beef and coconut milk to the mixture. Continue to simmer for 5 minutes, then add chilies, basil and kaffir lime leaves. Serve hot.

Serves 1 to 2

Soups are more than just first courses at a Thai table. They are sipped throughout a meal along with other dishes and play an important role in creating the essential blend of flavors which is so central to Thai cuisine.

◁ Shrimp Dtom Yam

(Dtom Yam Gung)

5 whole shrimp • 2 cups (500 ml/1 pt 1 fl oz) water
2 stalks lemon grass • 3 bird's eye chilies
5 slices galangal • 2 coriander roots, scraped
1 kaffir lime leaf, torn • 1 tsp dtom yam stock (made
from stock cubes) • 3 straw mushrooms, halved
2 cherry tomatoes, halved • 2 tsp fish sauce
1 tbsp lime juice • pinch of salt • 4 coriander leaves

Shell and devein the shrimp, keeping the tails
intact. Reserve the heads and shells. In a pot,
bring the water to a boil, then add the shrimp
heads and shells. Simmer for 5 minutes.
Remove the shrimp shells and return the water
to boil. Bruise the chilies and lemon grass
separately with a mortar and pestle, then add
them, together with the galangal, coriander
roots, kaffir leaf and dtom yam broth to the
boiling soup. Reduce heat and simmer for 2
minutes. Add the shrimp, mushrooms and
tomatoes and simmer for another 4 to 5
minutes. Remove from heat and season with
fish sauce, lime juice and salt. Garnish with
coriander leaves to serve.

Serves 1 to 2

▽ Hot & Sour Soup with Shredded Chicken & Lemon Grass (Dtom Jiw Gai)

2 cups (500 ml/1 pt 1 fl oz) chicken stock (see Basics)
pinch of salt • pinch of grated palm sugar • 4 slices galangal
2 stalks lemon grass • 3 red shallots • 2 kaffir lime leaves, torn
7 oz (200 g) small chicken drumsticks and chicken wings
3 tbsp lime juice • 2 tbsp fish sauce • 4 bird's eye chilies
1 tbsp coriander leaves

Bring the chicken stock to a boil and season with salt and palm sugar.
Add the galangal, lemon grass, shallots and kaffir lime leaves. Simmer for
3 minutes, then add the chicken. Simmer for 5 more minutes or until
chicken is tender. Remove the chicken and shred coarsely when cool.
Strain the stock and return to boil on medium heat. In a large bowl,
combine the lime juice, fish sauce and chilies. Add the shredded chicken,
then pour the boiling stock over this mixture. Garnish with the coriander
leaves to serve.

Serves 1 to 2

▷ Chicken & Lemon Grass Soup

(Dtom Khaa Gai)

½ cup (125 ml/4¼ fl oz) chicken stock (see Basics) • 1 cup (250 ml/8½ fl oz) coconut milk
1 cup (250 ml/8½ fl oz) coconut cream • 3 red shallots • 2 stalks lemon grass, chopped
2 kaffir lime leaves, torn • 1 coriander root, scraped • 2 to 3 bird's eye chilies • 8 slices galangal
2½ tbsp fish sauce • 2 tbsp lime juice • 1 tsp white sugar • 5 to 6 small mushrooms, halved
3½ oz (100 g) skinless chicken breasts, sliced • handful of coriander leaves, chopped
3 dried red chilies, fried

Combine the chicken stock, coconut milk and coconut cream in a wok and bring to a boil on medium heat. Add the shallots, lemon grass, lime leaves, coriander roots, chilies and galangal. Reduce the heat and simmer for 2 to 3 minutes. Season with fish sauce, lime juice and sugar. Add the mushrooms and chicken. Simmer for 2 more minutes or until the chicken is cooked but still tender. Garnish with the coriander leaves and fried dried red chilies to serve.

Serves 1 to 2

◁ Dried Shrimp, Pumpkin & Coconut Soup (Gaeng Dtom Gati Fak Tong)

½ cup (125 ml/4¼ fl oz) chicken stock (see Basics)
2 cups (500 ml/1 pt 1 fl oz) coconut milk • ¼ tsp salt • pinch of white sugar
⅝ cup (100 g/3½ oz) pumpkin, cubed • 5 shrimp, shelled and deveined
pinch of white pepper

PASTE ▷ 1 tbsp dried shrimp • 4 red shallots, chopped
3 coriander roots, scraped and chopped • 8 white peppercorns
pinch of salt

To prepare the paste, combine all the paste ingredients and pound with a mortar and pestle until smooth. In a hot wok, combine the stock with the coconut milk in a pot and bring to a boil. Season with salt and sugar. Add the paste to the stock and bring to a boil. Reduce the heat, then add the pumpkin cubes and shrimp. Simmer until the pumpkin is tender. Season with pepper to serve.

Serves 1 to 2

◁ Spicy Red Shrimp Curry (Chu Chee Gung)

1½ cups (375 ml/12¾ fl oz) coconut milk
2 tbsp red curry paste (see Basics)
1 tsp grated palm sugar • 3 tbsp fish sauce
2 tbsp chicken stock (see Basics)
6 medium shrimp, shelled and deveined with tails intact
2 kaffir lime leaves, shredded
1 long red chili, deseeded and sliced lengthwise

In a wok, warm the coconut milk over medium heat, then add the red curry paste and fry until fragrant. Season with palm sugar and fish sauce. Add the chicken stock and simmer until the mixture is reduced to a thick curry. Add the shrimp and 1 shredded kaffir lime leaf. Mix well and simmer for 5 more minutes. Garnish with the red chili and remaining shredded kaffir lime leaf to serve.

Serves 1 to 2

◁ Green Chicken Curry (Gaeng Gwio Warn Gai)

½ cup (125 ml/4¼ fl oz) coconut milk
1 cup (250 ml/8½ fl oz) coconut cream
2 tbsp green curry paste (see Basics)
2 tsp grated palm sugar • 1 tbsp fish sauce
3½ oz (100 g) skinless chicken thigh meat
3 kaffir lime leaves, torn
2 small eggplants, cut into sections
1 long red chili, sliced diagonally
handful of Thai basil leaves

Pour the coconut milk and coconut cream into a wok and bring to a boil. Add the curry paste and mix well. Add the palm sugar and fish sauce and cook for 1 to 2 minutes or until fragrant. Add the chicken, lime leaves and eggplants, and simmer for 2 to 3 minutes or until the chicken is cooked but still tender. Garnish with the chili and basil leaves to serve.

Serves 1 to 2

Sides

Thai side dishes are not mere accompaniments to the main meal, but play an important complementary role in maintaining the balance and harmony between the main dishes. They range from simple stir-fries to more elaborate creations which can relieve or enhance the characteristic piquancy of a typical Thai meal.

▷ Stir-Fried Asparagus with Shrimp (Pat Nor Mai Farang Gab Gung)

2 cloves garlic • pinch of salt • 2 tbsp oil • 3½ oz (100 g) young asparagus
1 tsp minced garlic • 4 shrimp, shelled and deveined with tails intact
1 tsp light soy sauce • 1 tsp oyster sauce • pinch of white sugar
pinch of white pepper • 2 tbsp chicken stock (see Basics) or water

Mix the garlic and salt well in a mortar then pound until
fine with the pestle. Heat the oil in a wok until very
hot, then add the garlic mixture, asparagus
and minced garlic. Stir-fry for about 3 to 4
minutes. Add the shrimp, soy sauce,
oyster sauce, sugar, white pepper
and chicken stock or water.
Simmer for 2 minutes
or until the shrimp
are cooked.

Serves 1 to 2

▽ Market Roast Chicken (Gai Yang)

5 coriander roots, scraped and chopped • 10 cloves garlic, chopped • 1 tbsp ground white peppercorns
3 stalks lemon grass (white sections only), chopped • pinch of salt • 1 tbsp soy sauce • 2 tbsp oyster sauce
1 tsp grated palm sugar • 1 medium chicken • steamed glutinous rice (see Basics)

Using a mortar and pestle, pound the coriander roots, garlic, peppercorns, lemon grass and salt into
a fine paste. Add the soy sauce, oyster sauce and palm sugar and mix well. Rub some of the paste
under the skin before marinating the chicken in this paste overnight. Grill or roast the chicken for 20
to 30 minutes or until the skin turns golden brown. Serve with steamed glutinous rice.

Serves 1 to 2

▷ Deep-Fried Squid with Garlic & Peppercorns

(Pla Meuk Tort Gratiam Prik Thai)

5¼ oz (150 g) squid, cleaned and scored • 2 heads garlic, unpeeled
3 coriander roots, scraped and chopped • 1 to 2 peppercorns • ¼ tsp salt
½ tsp white pepper • pinch of white sugar • ½ tbsp fish sauce
oil for deep-frying • 2 tbsp coriander leaves

Blanch the squid in boiling water for 1 to 2 minutes, then set aside. Using a mortar and pestle, pound the garlic, coriander roots and peppercorns into a rough paste. Remove the garlic skin, stem and base from the paste. Season with salt, pepper, sugar and fish sauce, then stir-fry the mixture on medium-high heat for 1 to 2 minutes. Deep-fry the cooked squid for 1 minute, then add the stir-fried garlic paste. Mix and stir-fry for 1 minute. Garnish with coriander leaves to serve.

Serves 1 to 2

△ Stir-Fried Asian Kale with Crispy Pork (Kana Muu Grob)

5¼ oz (150 g) Asian kale • 2 cloves garlic, coarsely chopped • 2 tbsp oil
3½ oz (100 g) ready-cooked crispy pork, cut into 1-in (2.5-cm) pieces
pinch of salt • pinch of white pepper • ¼ tsp sugar • 1 tbsp oyster sauce
4 tbsp chicken stock (see Basics) • 1 long red chili, deseeded and sliced

Prepare the Asian kale by removing the leaves and trimming the stems,
then cutting the stems into 3-in (7.5-cm) pieces. In a hot wok, fry the
garlic in the oil until fragrant, then add the Asian kale and pork, and stir-fry
for 2 to 3 minutes. Add the remaining ingredients, reduce heat and stir-fry
for another 2 minutes.

Serves 1 to 2

▽ Deep-Fried Chicken with Lemon Grass (Gai Tod Ta Krai)

1 tsp oyster sauce • 1 tsp light soy sauce • 1 tsp white sugar • 1 tsp fish sauce
1 tbsp freshly brewed lemon grass infusion • 5¼ oz (150 g) chicken breast, sliced
2 stalks lemon grass, finely chopped • 2 kaffir lime leaves, torn • oil for deep-frying

Mix the oyster sauce, soy sauce, sugar, fish sauce and infusion in a bowl.
Marinate the chicken in this mixture for 2 hours. Deep-fry the lemon grass
and kaffir leaves in the oil until crispy, then remove with a strainer and set
aside. Deep-fry the marinated chicken in the same oil until cooked but still
tender. Remove with a strainer. Garnish with the deep-fried lemon grass
and kaffir lime leaves to serve.

Serves 1 to 2

▷Fried Rice with Crabmeat

(Khao Pat Bpuu)

2 tbsp oil • 1 tsp minced garlic • pinch of salt • 1 egg
1 cup (90 g/3⅛ oz) steamed jasmine rice • 1 tsp light soy sauce
1 tsp oyster sauce • pinch of white sugar • 1 tbsp finely chopped spring onion
1 tbsp finely chopped white onion • 1 tbsp finely chopped carrot
½ cup (70 g/2½ oz) crabmeat, shredded • 1 tsp chopped coriander leaves
1 lime wedge • ½ small carrot, sliced and deep-fried

Heat the oil in a very hot wok. Fry the garlic with the salt in the oil until fragrant.
Crack in the egg and allow the whites to firm up before scrambling. Add the rice,
spreading it around the pan, and reduce the heat. Season with soy sauce, oyster
sauce and sugar. Stir-fry gently, tossing well. Add the spring onion, white onion, finely
chopped carrot and crabmeat, and cook for 2 minutes. Garnish with chopped
coriander, lime wedge and deep-fried carrot to serve.

Serves 1 to 2

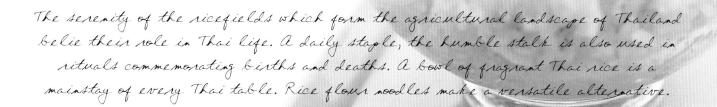

*The serenity of the ricefields which form the agricultural landscape of Thailand
belie their role in Thai life. A daily staple, the humble stalk is also used in
rituals commemorating births and deaths. A bowl of fragrant Thai rice is a
mainstay of every Thai table. Rice flour noodles make a versatile alternative.*

▽ Pineapple Fried Rice (Khao Pat Sapparot)

1 tsp minced garlic • pinch of salt
1 tbsp unsalted butter • 1 tbsp chopped onion
1 tsp curry powder • 4 tbsp coconut milk
4 shrimp, shelled and deveined • 1 tsp white sugar
2 tsp light soy sauce • 1 tsp oyster sauce
2 tbsp diced pineapple • 1 tbsp raisins
1½ cups (135 g/4¾ oz) cooked rice
1 tsp chopped spring onion
1 tbsp coriander leaves • pinch of white pepper

Heat oil in a very hot wok. Fry the garlic and salt in the butter until fragrant. Add the onion and curry powder and mix well. Add the coconut milk and shrimp and simmer for 3 minutes. Season with sugar, soy sauce and oyster sauce. Stir, then add the pineapple, raisins and rice. Reduce the heat and stir-fry for another 2 minutes, mixing well. Garnish with spring onion and coriander. Sprinkle with pepper to serve.

Serves 1 to 2

▷ Fried Rice Noodles (Pat Thai)

1 cup (100 g/2⅞ oz) dried thin rice noodles
1 tbsp chopped red shallots • 1 tbsp crushed garlic
1 tbsp oil • 1 egg • 1 tbsp beancurd
1 tbsp shredded white radish • 1 tsp dried shrimp
¼ tsp roasted chili powder • handful of bean sprouts
2 bunches Chinese chives, chopped
1 tbsp crushed roasted peanuts • 1 lime wedge

SAUCE ▷ 1 tbsp grated palm sugar
1 tbsp white sugar • 1 tbsp tamarind juice
1 tbsp fish sauce

Soak the rice noodles in cold water for about 1 hour or until soft. Drain and set aside. To prepare the sauce, simmer the palm sugar, white sugar, tamarind juice and fish sauce in a pan until dissolved. Set aside. In a wok, fry the shallots and garlic in the oil over medium heat until fragrant. Crack in the egg, reduce the heat and stir. Mix in the beancurd, white radish and dried shrimp, then add the noodles. Turn up the heat and stir-fry for 1 minute. Add the prepared sauce and chili powder, and simmer for 1 minute. Finally add most of the bean sprouts and chives and cook for 1 minute. Serve on a plate and top with crushed peanuts and bean sprouts. Garnish with lime wedge.

Serves 1 to 2

◁ Shrimp Paste Rice with Sweet Pork

(Khao Kluk Gapi)

2 tbsp oil • ½ tbsp minced garlic • ½ tbsp shrimp paste • 1 cup (90 g/3⅛ oz) cooked rice
½ cup (80 g/2¾ oz) sweet pork • ½ cup (80 g/2¾ oz) sliced omelette • 2 tbsp dried shrimp, deep-fried
3 tbsp sliced red shallots • ½ cup (80 g/2¾ oz) sliced green mango • 1 tbsp sliced long beans
½ small cucumber, sliced • ½ lime

SWEET PORK (MUU WARN) ▷ 1¾ oz (50 g) pork belly, sliced • 2 tbsp chicken stock (see Basics)
2 tbsp palm sugar • 2 tsp fish sauce • ½ tsp dark soy sauce

To prepare the sweet pork, simmer the pork belly in chicken stock until tender. Drain and slice the pork into small pieces when cool. Heat the palm sugar in a heavy saucepan until it caramelizes. Add the fish sauce, dark soy sauce and a little of the stock, mix well then add the pork and simmer for 15 minutes. Add oil to a hot wok and stir-fry the minced garlic until fragrant. Add the shrimp paste and continue stir-frying. Add the cooked rice and toss well. Serve warm with the sweet pork, sliced omelette, dried shrimp, shallots, green mango and lime on the side.

Serves 1 to 2

▷ Stir-Fried Rice Noodles with Asian Kale & Chicken

(Gai Pat Sii Uuu)

1½ tbsp oil • 1 tsp finely chopped garlic
2½ oz (70 g) chicken thigh fillet, sliced
2½ oz (70 g) Asian kale, trimmed and cut into 1½-in (3.75-cm) lengths
3½ oz (100 g) broad rice noodles • 1 egg • 1 tsp white sugar
1 tsp oyster sauce • 1 tsp dark soy sauce • 1 tbsp light soy sauce
2 tsp chicken stock (see Basics) • 1 tbsp coriander leaves
1 long red chili, sliced • pinch of white pepper

In a wok on high heat, stir-fry the garlic in oil until golden brown. Add the chicken and continue to stir-fry until chicken is almost cooked. Add the Asian kale and noodles, and cook for 3 minutes. Add the egg and stir-fry for 1 minute. Add the soy sauces, sugar and chicken stock. Mix well and cook for 1 more minute. Serve sprinkled with coriander, chili and pepper.

Serves 1 to 2

▷ Steamed Rice with Basil Chicken & Fried Egg

(Khao Pat Kra-Praow Gai Khai Dow)

1 egg • 1 tbsp oil • ½ tbsp minced bird's eye chilies
½ tbsp minced garlic
⅓ cup (100 g/3½ oz) minced chicken breast
½ tsp oyster sauce • 1 tsp fish sauce
½ tsp sugar • 2 tbsp chicken stock (see Basics)
1 long red chili, crushed and sliced
handful of Thai basil leaves, deep-fried
1 cup (90 g/3⅛ oz) cooked rice

Break egg into a bowl, then gently pour into a wok with oil at high heat. Spread the egg by rolling the wok gently and fry for 30 seconds, then gently turn over and fry for another 30 seconds. Remove and set aside. Retain the oil in the wok and add the chilies and garlic. Stir-fry for 30 seconds, then reduce the heat to medium and add the chicken. Stir-fry for 30 seconds, then add the oyster sauce, fish sauce, sugar and chicken stock. Mix well and add the red chilies and basil. Stir-fry for 1 more minute before removing from heat. Serve the chicken on the side of the steamed rice. Top the rice with the fried egg.

Serves 1 to 2

△ Stir-Fried Rice Noodles with Tuna, Broccoli & Basil

(Pat Kee Mao Sen Yai)

3½ oz (100 g) broad rice noodles • 1 tbsp cooking oil • ½ tsp dark soy sauce
1 tbsp finely chopped garlic • ⅓ cup (70 g/2½ oz) canned white tuna flakes
1 tbsp chopped bird's eye chilies • 1 tbsp chicken stock (see Basics)
¼ cup (45 g/1½ oz) carrot, cut into 1-in (2.5-cm) pieces
¼ cup (45 g/1½ oz) Asian kale, trimmed and cut • 3 ears baby corn
¼ cup (45 g/1½ oz) broccoli florets • 1 tbsp light soy sauce • 1 tbsp oyster sauce
½ tbsp fish sauce • ½ tbsp white sugar • 2 srida tomatoes, halved
2 stems green peppercorns • handful of basil leaves, deep-fried

Fry noodles in a wok with oil and dark soy sauce. Set aside. Heat the remaining oil in a hot wok and stir-fry the garlic until fragrant. Reduce heat and add tuna, chilies and chicken stock. Stir-fry with garlic. Add noodles and vegetables. Stir-fry for 3 minutes. Season with sauces and sugar. Toss and add tomatoes and peppercorns. Serve with deep-fried basil.

Serves 1 to 2

▷ Crispy Rice Noodles with Pork & Gravy (Laat Nar Muu)

3½ oz (100 g) fresh flat rice noodles • ½ tsp dark soy sauce
2 ears baby corn, sliced lengthwise • ⅞ oz (25 g) broccoli florets
⅞ oz (25 g) carrot, cut into 2-in (5-cm) pieces
⅞ oz (25 g) Asian kale, chopped and trimmed • oil for frying
½ tbsp oil • 1 clove garlic, minced • 2½ oz (70 g) pork, thinly sliced
2 cups (500 ml/1 pt 1 fl oz) chicken stock (see Basics) • 3 mushrooms, halved
1 tsp yellow bean sauce • 1 tbsp light soy sauce • 1 tsp beaten egg
2 tbsp tapioca flour mixed with 1 tbsp water

Season the noodles with dark soy sauce and set aside for 10 minutes.
Blanch the baby corn, broccoli, carrots and Asian kale. Set aside. Heat
cooking oil in a wok and stir-fry the noodles until slightly crisp, then remove
and keep warm. Heat ½ tbsp of oil and fry the garlic until fragrant, then
add the pork and stir-fry until the garlic turns golden brown. Add the stock,
mushrooms and vegetables, then season with the yellow bean sauce and
light soy sauce. Add the egg and tapioca flour paste and stir until the
gravy thickens. Pour the gravy over the crisp noodles to serve.

Serves 1 to 2

◁ Red Curry Fried Rice with Deep-Fried Catfish

(Khao Pat Nahm Prik Pla Duk Fuu)

1 (400 g/14 oz) smoked catfish, skinned, deboned and chopped • oil for deep-frying
2 tbsp oil • 4 tsp red curry paste (see Basics) • 8 tbsp coconut cream
2 cups (180 g/6⅜ oz) cooked rice • 2 tsp grated palm sugar • 2 tsp salt
4 shallots, thinly sliced • 1½ cups (230 g/8¼ oz) shredded green mango
2 lime wedges

Deep-fry the chopped catfish in hot oil until golden and crisp. Set aside to
cool. Heat oil in a very hot wok and stir-fry the red curry paste until fragrant.
Add the coconut cream, sugar and salt. Reduce heat and simmer for 1
minute. Add the rice and mix thoroughly, stir-frying for 2 minutes. Top the rice
with the fried catfish and garnish with shallots, mango and lime wedges.

Serves 1 to 2

Though of Chinese origin, egg noodles are a basic constituent of countless fast-food dishes offered by street vendors and restaurants in Thailand.

▷ Egg Noodles with Barbecued Pork (Ba Mee Muu Daeng)

1 Chinese mustard cabbage • handful of bean sprouts
1 ball Chinese egg noodles • 1 tsp minced garlic, deep-fried
50 g barbecued pork • 4 wontons • pinch of white pepper
1 cup (250 ml/8½ fl oz) chicken stock • 1 tsp sliced spring onion and cilantro

BARBECUED PORK ▷　1 lb (455 g) pork
2 tbsp sugar • 1 tsp salt • 2 tbsp light soy sauce
1 tsp Chinese five-spice powder • 1 tsp honey (optional)
2 tsp roast red pork seasoning mix (optional)

To prepare the barbecued pork, cut the pork into long 2-in (5-cm) wide pieces. Marinate with sugar, soy sauce, salt, pork seasoning and five-spice powder overnight. Preheat the oven at 350° F (177° C) and bake for 1 hour on a tray or aluminum foil. When done, the pork should be reddish, firm and dry, but not burnt. Boil water in a pot. Cut the Chinese mustard cabbage into bite-sized pieces and blanch in the water. If you prefer the bean sprouts cooked, blanch them and set aside. Cook the noodles in boiling water for 1 minute, using chopsticks to separate the strands. Add 1 tsp of minced deep-fried garlic to the noodles and toss well, ensuring that the noodles do not stick together. Slice the barbecued pork thinly and arrange the slices with the wontons on top of the noodles. Add the bean sprouts and pepper. Pour the stock over the noodles and sliced pork. Garnish with spring onion and cilantro.

Serves 1 to 2

▽ Egg Noodles with Spicy Minced Pork

(Ba Mee Tom Yam Muu Sab)

1 cup (250 ml/8½ fl oz) chicken stock (see Basics) • 1 ball Chinese egg noodles • 4 fish balls
⅓ cup (50 g/1¾ oz) minced pork • ⅝ cup (50 g/1¾ oz) bean sprouts • 1½ tbsp chili paste
1 tbsp roasted peanuts, crushed • 2 tbsp lime juice • 1 tsp chili powder • 2 tsp fish sauce
1 tsp sugar • 1 tsp minced garlic, deep-fried (see Basics) • 1 stalk Chinese celery, chopped

Bring the stock to a boil, then set aside. Boil water in a pot and cook the noodles
in it for 1 minute, separating the strands with chopsticks. Remove the noodles
with a strainer to a bowl. Using the same boiling water, blanch the fish balls, pork
and bean sprouts, and add to the noodles. Add the chili paste and peanuts.
Season with lime juice, chili powder, fish sauce and sugar. Pour in the stock
and garnish with deep-fried garlic and chopped Chinese celery.

Serves 1 to 2

◁ Egg Noodles with Marinated Chicken

(Ba Mee Gai Toon)

2 cups (500 ml/1 pt 1 fl oz) water
4 dried shiitake mushrooms, soaked and washed
1 lb 1⅝ oz (500 g) chicken drumsticks
2 slices Chinese yam • 6 wolfberries
1 coriander root • 3 cloves garlic, crushed
1 Chinese star anise • ½ cinnamon stick
1½ tbsp rock sugar • 1½ tbsp oyster sauce
½ tbsp dark soy sauce • 1 tbsp light soy sauce
½ tsp black peppercorns • 1 ball Chinese egg noodles
⅝ cup (50 g/1¾ oz) bean sprouts, blanched
1 tbsp finely chopped spring onion
1 tbsp finely chopped coriander leaves
1 tbsp minced garlic, deep-fried • pinch of pepper

Boil the water, then add mushrooms, chicken,
herbs and garlic. Season with spices, sugar and
sauces, and simmer for 1 hour. Boil the noodles
for 1 minute. Strain and place in a bowl. Add the
bean sprouts. Slice the chicken and place with
the mushrooms on the noodles. Pour the stock
over. Garnish with spring onion, coriander and
garlic. Sprinkle with pepper.

Serves 1 to 2

Thai Muslim

The predominantly Muslim region of southern Thailand has given birth to a cuisine that wholeheartedly embraces the liberal use of dried spices. These dishes would have been familiar to the Muslim weaving community which produced Jim Thompson's silks, providing them with flavorful sustenance for the day's labors.

▷ Muslim-Style Noodles

(Kuay Tiew Issalam)

2 shallots, chopped • 5 dried bird's eye chilies, chopped
1 cup (250 ml/8½ fl oz) coconut milk • ⅓ cup (83 ml/3 fl oz) coconut cream
1 bay leaf, torn • pinch of ground cumin
5¼ oz (150 g) beef sirloin, thinly sliced into 1½-in- (3.75-cm-) long pieces
1 cup (100 g/2⅞ oz) rice noodles • 3½ oz (100 g) Asian kale
2 tbsp tamarind juice • 2 tbsp sugar • 2 tbsp sweet soybean sauce
3 tbsp fish sauce

Pound the shallots and chilies to a smooth paste with a mortar and pestle.
Combine the paste, coconut milk and cream in a wok and bring to a boil.
Reduce heat and simmer for 2 minutes. Add the bay leaf and cumin,
then add the beef and let the mixture simmer for 3 minutes. Add the
rice noodles, kai lan, tamarind juice, sugar and sweet soybean
sauce. Season with fish sauce and serve.

Serves 1 to 2

◁ Muslim Oxtail Soup

(Sup Hang Wua)

6 lbs (2.5 kg) oxtail, cut into segments • 5 white onions, chopped • pinch of salt
5 cups (1.2 L/2 pts 9 fl oz) ginger water • 2 bird's eye chilies • pinch of white pepper
1 tbsp chopped coriander leaves • 3 tbsp sliced shallots, deep-fried

CURRY POWDER ▷   1 tbsp black peppercorns • 20 Thai cardamom pods
1 tbsp cloves • 3 tbsp cumin seeds • 3 tbsp coriander seeds • 3 tbsp chili powder
3 long red chilies • 1 tbsp tamarind juice • 5 tbsp ground dried ginger
3½ tbsp ground tumeric

To prepare the curry powder, quickly dry-roast the whole
spices in a pan, then pound to a fine powder with a
mortar and pestle. Add the ground ingredients
and mix together well, then pass the mixture
through a sieve.

Wash the oxtail and place in a pot with
the onions. Add the salt, 4½ tbsp
of the curry powder and ginger
water. Bring to a boil then reduce
the heat and simmer for 3 to 4
hours or until tender. When the
stock cools, debone the
oxtail and return the meat to
the soup. Reheat gently. Add
the chilies, pepper, coriander
and deep-fried shallots.
Serve warm.

Serves 1 to 2

▷ Beef Mussaman Curry

(Gaeng Mussaman Neua)

1 cup (250 ml/8½ fl oz) coconut cream
3½ oz (100 g) beef sirloin, cubed
2 cups (500 ml/1 pt 1 fl oz) coconut milk
3 tbsp mussaman curry paste (see Basics)
2 cardamom seeds, roasted • 1 tbsp roasted peanuts
3 small potatoes, peeled and quartered
1 small sweet white onion, quartered
2 bay leaves, torn • ½ tsp salt
1 tbsp grated palm sugar • 2 tbsp fish sauce
2 shallots, sliced and deep-fried • oil for frying

In a wok, bring the coconut cream to a boil. Add
the beef and simmer for about 1½ hours or until
the meat is tender. Stir-fry the coconut milk and
curry paste over medium heat for 5 minutes. Add
the coconut cream mixture and simmer for 30
minutes. Add the cardamom seeds, peanuts,
potatoes, onion and bay leaves. Simmer for another
10 to 15 minutes or until the potatoes are tender.
Season with the salt, sugar and fish sauce and bring to a
boil. Remove from heat and garnish with shallots.

Serves 1 to 2

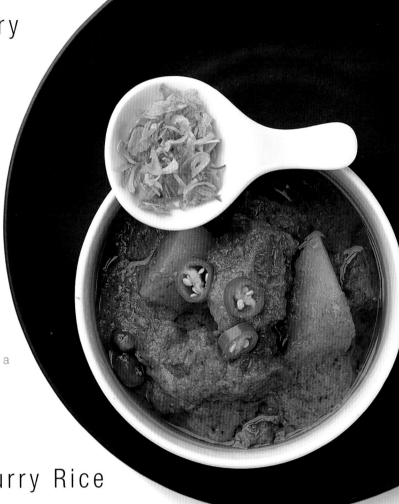

◁ Steamed Chicken Curry Rice

(Khao Mok Gai)

3 red shallots, sliced • 3 tbsp cooking oil • 1 chicken drumstick • 2 tbsp curry powder
1 cup (200 g/7 oz) uncooked jasmine rice • 2 cups (500 ml/1 pt 1 fl oz) chicken stock (see Basics)
6 to 7 cardamom seeds • 3 bay leaves

In a wok on high heat, fry the shallots in the oil until crisp, then remove from the oil with a strainer
and set aside. Add the chicken, curry powder and rice to the shallot oil and stir-fry over medium-high
heat. Mix well. Add 1 cup (250 ml/8½ fl oz) of the chicken stock to this mixture and stir for about 5
minutes, until the rice is almost cooked. Transfer everything to a rice pot and slowly add the
remaining chicken stock, cardamom seeds and bay leaves. Bring to a boil, then reduce the heat
and cover the pot. Cook for 10 minutes. Garnish with fried shallots to serve.

Serves 1 to 2

Thai Continental

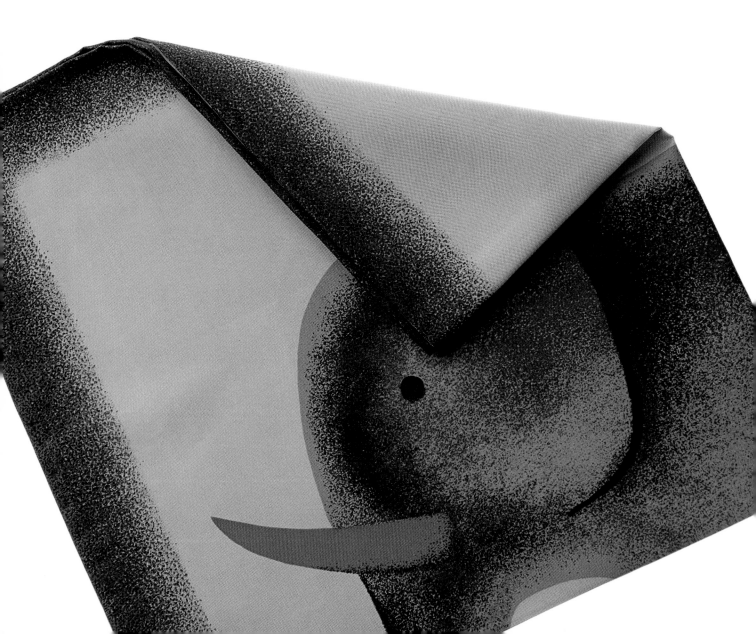

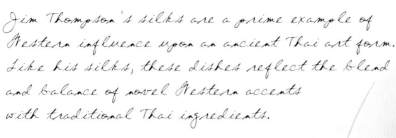

Jim Thompson's silks are a prime example of Western influence upon an ancient Thai art form. Like his silks, these dishes reflect the blend and balance of novel Western accents with traditional Thai ingredients.

▷ Fettuccine with Chicken Curry

(Fettuccine Khao Soi Gai)

4 oz (120 g) cooked fettuccine
1 cup (250 ml/8½ fl oz) coconut milk
1 tbsp red curry paste (see Basics)
5 g (⅛ oz) shallots, finely diced
3½ oz (100 g) chicken fillet, skinned and sliced
1 tsp grated palm sugar • 1 tsp fish sauce
½ tsp roasted chili paste • 2 tbsp diced shallots
1 tbsp fried red chilies • ½ lime • oil for frying

Deep-fry the fettuccine noodles until crispy and golden brown. Drain and set aside. In a medium-hot wok simmer the coconut milk until it thickens. Add the curry paste and fry until fragrant. Add the shallots and chicken, then simmer for 2 to 3 minutes. Season with the palm sugar, fish sauce and chili paste. Pour the curry over the fettuccine and garnish with shallots, chilies and lime to serve.

Serves 1 to 2

▽ Grilled Pork Sandwich

(Sandwich Muu Yang)

4 slices (300 g/10½ oz) pork neck • 2 tsp sugar • 2 tsp oyster sauce
2 tsp light soy sauce • 1 tsp chopped garlic • 2 coriander roots, chopped
ground black pepper to taste • 4 slices bread, toasted • 2 lettuce leaves
4 slices cucumber • 2 leaves iceberg lettuce • 4 slices tomato
1 cup (220 ml/7½ fl oz) chili sauce

Marinate the pork neck in the sugar, oyster sauce, soy sauce, garlic,
coriander root and ground black pepper for 1 hour. Grill the pork over hot
charcoal or pan-fry the pork in oil, until the meat is cooked but still tender.
Sandwich the pork between the vegetables and bread and serve with chili
sauce on the side.

Serves 1 to 2

◁ Shrimp Dtom Yam Linguine

(Linguine Dtom Yam Gung)

3½ oz (100 g) linguine • pinch of salt
1 tbsp olive oil • 1 stalk lemon grass, chopped
2 kaffir lime leaves, torn
4 button mushrooms, quartered
1 tomato, quartered
3 shrimp with tails intact, blanched
¼ cup (62.5 ml/2⅛ fl oz) chicken stock (see Basics)
3 tbsp whipping cream • ½ tbsp white sugar
½ tsp roasted chili powder • ½ tbsp lemon juice
large pinch of freshly grated Parmesan cheese
pinch of Thai parsley

Cook the linguine in salted boiling water
until al dente. Drain and cover. Set aside.
In a saucepan, heat the olive oil on medium-low
heat. Add the lemon grass, kaffir lime leaves
mushrooms and tomato. Simmer for 2 to 3
minutes. Add the chicken stock and cook for
1 minute. Add the whipping cream, sugar, chili
powder and lemon juice. Stir and simmer.
Add the cooked linguine and shrimp. Toss
with Parmesan cheese. Serve with parsley.

Serves 1 to 2

▷ Spaghetti with Tuna

(Spaghetti Pat Kee Mao)

3½ oz (100 g) spaghetti
2 tbsp oil • 1 tbsp minced garlic
5 red bird's eye chilies, bruised
2 stems Thai green peppercorns
3/8 oz (10 g) young carrot, cut into
1½-in (3.75-cm) quarter sections
3/8 oz (10 g) broccoli, trimmed
3/8 oz (10 g) cauliflower florets
3/8 oz (10 g) ears baby corn, trimmed
3/8 oz (10 g) Asian kale, trimmed and cut into
1½-in (3.75-cm) pieces
¼ tsp dark soy sauce • 1 tsp light soy sauce
2 tsp oyster sauce • ¼ tsp white sugar
1 tbsp chicken stock (see Basics)
1/3 cup (70 g/2½ oz) canned white tuna flakes
1 small tomato, cleaned and quartered
4 Thai basil leaves, deep-fried

Cook the spaghetti in salted boiling water until
al dente. Heat the oil in a wok and stir-fry the
garlic until fragrant. Add the chilies, peppercorns
and the rest of the vegetables. Cook for 2 to 3
minutes or until tender. Season with soy sauce,
oyster sauce and white sugar, then add the
chicken stock and simmer for 1 to 2 minutes.
Add the cooked spaghetti, tuna and tomatoes.
Toss well and garnish with the deep-fried basil
leaves to serve.

Serves 1 to 2

▷ Spaghetti with Spicy Chicken Salad (Spaghetti Larb Gai)

3½ oz (100 g) spaghetti
½ cup (125 ml/4¼ fl oz) chicken stock (see Basics)
5/8 cup (120 g/4¼ oz) minced chicken
1½ tbsp fish sauce • 2 tbsp lime juice
2½ tsp dried chili powder • ¾ tbsp sugar
1 tbsp ground roasted rice (see Basics)
1¾ oz (50 g) shallots, sliced
¾ oz (20 g) spring onion, sliced
3/8 oz (10 g) long-leaf coriander, chopped
2 dried chilies, fried
handful mint leaves, chopped

Cook the spaghetti in salted boiling water until
al dente. In a pasta pan, heat the olive oil and
stir-fry the minced chicken on medium heat for
1 minute. Add the chicken stock and reduce
until thick. Season with fish sauce, lime juice,
chili powder, sugar and ground roasted rice,
mixing well. Add the shallots, spring onion
and coriander, then mix well. Add the cooked
spaghetti and toss well. Garnish with mint
leaves and dried chilies to serve.

Serves 1 to 2

Desserts | Drinks

The origins of Thai desserts lie in worship and ceremony, with each ingredient bearing its own symbolic meaning. While these might now be lost, the intricacy of their design and freshness of the ingredients can still be savored.

△ Water Chestnut & Coconut Custard Cones (Ta-Ko Haew)

BASE ▷ 1 ½ cups (195 g/7 oz) rice flour • ¾ cup white sugar • 1 ½ cups (375 ml/12¾ fl oz) perfumed water (see Basics) • ¼ cup (25 g/⅞ oz) water chestnuts, cooked and diced

TOPPING ▷ 6 tbsp cornflour • 3 cups (750 ml/1 pt 9½ fl oz) coconut cream • ½ tsp salt ½ tsp white sugar • 10 4-by-8-in (10-by-20-cm) banana leaves, shaped into cones

In a medium saucepan, combine the flour and sugar. Add the perfumed water and mix well. Cook on medium heat until flour thickens. Add the water chestnuts, mix well and set aside. In a saucepan, combine the cornflour, salt and sugar. Pour in the coconut cream and bring the mixture to a boil on medium heat, stirring frequently. Reduce heat, simmer for 1 minute and transfer into banana-leaf cones. Let cool before serving.

Serves 1 to 2

▽ Pandanus Tapioca

(Saku Song Kreuang)

12 lychees • 1 cup (150 g/5⅓ oz) tapioca pearls • 3 pandanus leaves
½ cup (125 ml/4¼ fl oz) water • ½ cup (100 g/3½ oz) sugar
flesh of 1 young coconut, shredded • 2 tbsp coconut cream

Peel and halve the lychees, removing the seeds. Cook the tapioca pearls in boiling water for 15 minutes until almost transparent, stirring to prevent them from burning. Drain the pearls, then soak in cold water. Drain well. Blend the pandanus leaves in the water until smooth, then pass the mixture through a sieve and discard the pulp. Simmer the liquid for 2 minutes to remove its raw taste. Add the sugar, stir until completely dissolved, then add the coconut, lychees and cooked tapioca pearls. Mix well and top with coconut cream to serve.

Serves 8

▷ Glutinous Rice in Coconut Milk with Custard

(Khao Niao Nah Sang Kha-Ya)

½ tsp salt • ⅓ cup (60 g/2⅛ oz) sugar
1 cup (250 ml/8½ fl oz) coconut milk
1 cup (180 g/6⅜ oz) steamed glutinous rice
(see Basics)

CUSTARD ▷ 1 cup (250 ml/8½ fl oz) coconut milk
1 tbsp rice flour • 1 cup (20 g/7 oz) grated palm sugar
1 tbsp coconut cream • 1 banana or pandanus leaf
4 eggs

Dissolve the salt and sugar in the coconut milk and pass the mixture through a fine-mesh sieve. Bring it to a boil, stirring constantly to prevent lumps from forming, then remove from heat and set aside. Place the steamed glutinous rice in a bowl and pour in the coconut milk over the rice. Stir for about 5 minutes.
To prepare the custard, use a banana or pandanus leaf to beat the coconut milk, palm sugar and eggs together. Pass the mixture through a fine-mesh sieve, then pour it into a heat-proof mold. Steam for 25 to 30 minutes, then remove from heat and set aside to cool. Place some custard on the glutinous rice and top with coconut cream to serve.

Serves 1 to 2

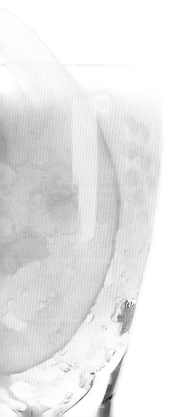

In larger cities like Bangkok and Chiang Mai, sophisticated Thais have developed a taste for many Western sweets that would have been rare or unknown a few decades ago. Thus such treats as cheese cake and ice creams with unusual flavorings are often found on menus otherwise devoted to purely Thai dishes.

◁ Mango Cheese Cake

CRUST ▷ 1½ cups (180 g/6½ oz) mocha cookies (see page 97)
¼ cup (50 g/1¾ oz) icing sugar • ¼ cup (50 g/1¾ oz) cocoa powder
¼ cup (50 g/1¾ oz) unsalted butter

CAKE ▷ 3 cups (700 g/1 lb 8½ oz) cream cheese
1 cup (225 g/8 oz) white sugar • 4 eggs • ½ cup (112.5 g/4 oz) sour cream
1½ tsp vanilla cream

FILLING ▷ 1⅓ cups (200 g/7 oz) fresh mango • 2 tbsp white sugar
2 tsp lemon juice

GLAZE ▷ 1 cup (250 ml/8½ fl oz) fresh whipped cream • 1 cup (135 g/4¾ oz)
almond slices, roasted • ½ cup (110 g/4 oz) apricot jam • ½ mango, sliced

Preheat the oven to 350° F (175° C). Butter and lightly flour an 8¾-in (22-cm) round metal cake mold or ring. Grind mocha cookies in processor to coarse crumbs. Add icing sugar, cocoa powder and unsalted butter. Blend until evenly moist. Press crumbs over the bottom of the prepared mold to ½-in (1.25-cm) thick. Bake crust for 5 to 6 minutes. Transfer to a rack to cool. Lower oven temperature to 325° F (160° C). To prepare the cake, use an electric mixer to beat the cream cheese in a large bowl until fluffy. Set aside.

To make the filling, combine the filling ingredients in a heavy saucepan. Cover and cook over medium to high heat until the sugar is dissolved and mangoes are tender. Using an electric mixer, beat cream cheese and sugar in a large bowl until fluffy. Beat in 1 egg at a time. Mix in sour cream and vanilla. Spoon a layer of the cream cheese mixture onto the crust, then spoon a layer of the mango compôte over the top of the cream cheese. Repeat until mango compôte is finished. Bake for about 1 hour in the oven at 325° F (160° C) until the cake puffs up, is cooked in the center and starts to turn brown. Remove from heat and place on a rack to cool. Remove the cake from the mold and chill overnight.

Remove cake from refrigerator. Using an electric mixer, beat whipped cream in a large bowl until fluffy. Using a spatula or palette knife, spread the whipped cream around the cake, then coat the whipped cream with the roasted almond slivers. Top with a spoonful of apricot jam and sliced mango to serve.

Serves 10

◁ Mocha Layer Cake with Chocolate-Rum Cream Filling

FILLING AND TOPPING ▷ 4 cups (1 L/1 pt 14 fl oz) whipping cream
¼ cup (60 g/2 oz) unsalted butter • ¼ cup (50 g/1⅔ oz) sugar
1 lb 6 oz (625 g) semisweet chocolate, finely chopped
⅓ cup (75 ml/2½ fl oz) dark Bacardi rum • 2 tsp vanilla essence
8 to 10 maraschino cherries • 8 to 10 white chocolate crisps

SYRUP ▷ ¼ cup (60 ml/2 fl oz) water • 2 tbsp sugar • 2 tbsp dark Bacardi rum

CAKE ▷ ⅔ cup (87 g/3 oz) all-purpose flour • ½ tsp baking soda
3 tbsp unsweetened cocoa powder • 1½ tsp vanilla essence
¾ tsp instant coffee granules • 3 large eggs, separated
¾ cup (155 g/5½ oz) sugar • ¼ tsp cream of tartar • ¼ tsp salt

To prepare the filling and topping, stir the whipping cream, butter and
sugar in a large heavy saucepan over medium-high heat until the sugar
dissolves and the cream starts to simmer. Remove from heat. Add all
but 2 oz (60 g) of the chocolate and whisk until well blended.
Whisk in the rum and vanilla essence. Transfer 1 cup (240 ml/8⅛ fl oz)
of this mixture to a small bowl and whisk in the remaining chocolate.
Set aside for use as topping. Cover and let stand at room temperature.
Transfer the rest of the chocolate mixture to a large bowl for the filling.
Chill for least 6 hours or up to 1 day until cold and thick.
To prepare the syrup, combine the water and sugar in a small saucepan
and stir over low heat until the sugar dissolves. Remove from heat and mix
in the rum. Cover and let stand for up to 1 day. Set aside.
To prepare the cake, preheat the oven at 350° F (175° C). Line the bottom
of an 8¾-in (22-cm) round metal cake mold with greaseproof paper and
brush the paper with butter. Sift the flour, cocoa powder and baking soda
into a small bowl. Set aside. Combine the vanilla essence and coffee
granules in a cup and stir to dissolve the coffee. Set aside.
Using an electric mixer, beat the egg yolks and ½ cup (100 g/3½ oz) of
the sugar in a medium bowl for 3 minutes or until the mixture is very thick
and pale. Whisk in the vanilla-coffee mixture. Set aside.
Using a clean dry whisk, beat the egg whites, cream of tartar and salt in a
large bowl until soft peaks form. Gradually add the remaining sugar,
beating until the mixture is stiff but not dry. Fold a third of this mixture into
the egg yolk mixture, then fold in half of the flour mixture.
Fold in half of the remaining egg white mixture, then fold in the leftover
flour mixture, followed by all the leftover egg white mixture. Transfer the
batter to the prepared mold and spread the mixture out evenly. Bake
for 18 minutes, or until the mixture rises and a metal skewer, when
inserted into the middle of the cake, comes out clean. Remove

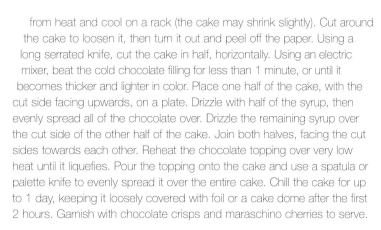

from heat and cool on a rack (the cake may shrink slightly). Cut around the cake to loosen it, then turn it out and peel off the paper. Using a long serrated knife, cut the cake in half, horizontally. Using an electric mixer, beat the cold chocolate filling for less than 1 minute, or until it becomes thicker and lighter in color. Place one half of the cake, with the cut side facing upwards, on a plate. Drizzle with half of the syrup, then evenly spread all of the chocolate over. Drizzle the remaining syrup over the cut side of the other half of the cake. Join both halves, facing the cut sides towards each other. Reheat the chocolate topping over very low heat until it liquefies. Pour the topping onto the cake and use a spatula or palette knife to evenly spread it over the entire cake. Chill the cake for up to 1 day, keeping it loosely covered with foil or a cake dome after the first 2 hours. Garnish with chocolate crisps and maraschino cherries to serve.

Serves 10

◁ Blueberry Cheese Cake

CRUST ▷ 1 1/2 cups (180 g/6 3/8 oz) Carmen's butter crescents, coarsely ground (see page 97) • 1/4 cup (50 g/1 3/4 oz) icing sugar 1/4 cup (50 g/1 3/4 oz) unsalted butter

CAKE ▷ 3 1/3 cups (750 g/1 lb 10 1/4 oz) cream cheese 1/2 cup (100 g/3 1/2 oz) sugar • 3 eggs • 1 1/2 tsp vanilla essence 3/4 cup (180 ml/6 fl oz) whipping cream

TOPPING ▷ 1 1/2 cups (330 g/11 5/8 oz) blueberry preserve

Preheat the oven at 350° F (175° C).
Butter and lightly flour an 8 3/4-in (22-cm) round metal cake mold or ring. To prepare crust, mix butter cookies with icing sugar and butter and blend until moist. Press mixture evenly over the bottom of the prepared mold and bake for 5 to 6 minutes. Transfer to a rack to cool. Lower oven temperature to 320° F (160° C). To prepare the cake, use an electric mixer to beat cream cheese and sugar in a large bowl until fluffy. Beat in 1 egg at a time, then mix in vanilla essence and whipping cream. Pour mixture over crust in mold, then place mold in a larger pan filled with water about 1-in (2.5-cm) deep. Bake for 1 to 1 1/2 hours until cake puffs up, is cooked in the center and starts to brown. Remove from heat and place on a rack to cool for at least 1 hour. Top the cake with the blueberry preserve and spread evenly with a palette knife. Keep chilled until ready to serve.

Serves 10

▷ Pandanus Ice Cream

4³⁄₈ oz (125 g) fresh pandanus leaves
1 cup (250 ml/8½ fl oz) water
6 egg yolks • ¾ cup (165 g/6oz) white sugar
1 cup (225 ml/7⅝ fl oz) whipping cream
4¼ cups (500 ml/1 pt 1 fl oz) milk
¼ cup (30 ml/1 fl oz) green food coloring

Blend the pandanus leaves and water in a food processor until smooth, then pass the mixture through a sieve and discard the pulp.
Whisk the egg yolks and sugar together until light and creamy, then add the whipping cream, milk and food coloring. Whisk to blend.
Fold the pandanus mixture into the cream and freeze. Serve when the mixture is frozen.

Makes 2½ pt (1.5 L)

▷ Thai Coconut Ice Cream

2 eggs • 1 cup (200 g/7 oz) white sugar
2 cups (470 ml/16 fl oz) whipping cream
2⅛ cups (500 ml/1 pt 1 fl oz) coconut cream
½ cup (115 g/4 oz) fresh jackfruit, chopped
½ cup (115 g/4 oz) fresh corn kernels, boiled
½ cup (115 g/4 oz) fresh coconut flesh, shredded
½ cup (115 g/4 oz) pandan dumpling, chopped

Whisk the eggs until light and fluffy. Add the sugar, a little at a time, and whisk until it is completely blended. Whisk in the whipping cream and coconut cream. Set aside.
Process the cream mixture in an ice-cream maker following the manufacturer's instructions. Blend in the jackfruit, corn, coconut and gelatin strips. Return to freezer and serve when the mixture is frozen.

Makes 2½ pt (1.5 L)

▷ Durian Ice Cream

2 eggs • 1 cup (200 g/7 oz) sugar • 2 cups (470 ml/16 fl oz) whipping cream
1½ cups (375 ml/12⅝ fl oz) milk • 1 lb 1⅝oz (500 g) fresh durian

Whisk the eggs until light and fluffy. Add the sugar, a little at a time, and whisk until it is completely blended. Whisk in the milk and whipping cream. Set aside. Pull apart the fresh durian and lightly mash in a small pan until fragrant. Process the cream mixture in an ice-cream maker following the manufacturer's instructions. Blend in the mashed durian flesh when the ice cream is frozen. Return to freezer and serve when the mixture is stiff. (Note: a well-ripened durian will impart a deliciously strong flavor.)

Makes 2½ pt (1.5 L)

Sweets to placate the gods now find their way to the table at the end of a Thai meal, surprising with their wide palette of colors and creativity of production.

▷Thai Kah-Fe

1 double espresso
2 tbsp sweetened condensed milk

Spoon the condensed milk into a glass of
double espresso and allow the milk to settle
at the bottom of the glass. Serve hot with a
coffee spoon and stir to combine the coffee
and milk before drinking.

Serves 1

◁ Mocha Cookies

2½ cups (315 g/11 oz) cake flour • ½ tsp salt
1 tsp baking powder • 1 tsp baking soda
1 cup (200 g/7 oz) brown sugar
1 cup (200 g/7 oz) white sugar
8 oz (225 g) unsalted butter
¼ cup (50 g/1¾ oz) white butter
2 eggs • ¾ cup (85 g/3 oz) walnuts
4 tbsp coffee powder
½ cup (65 g/3 oz) cocoa powder
1½ cups (170 g/6 oz) chocolate chips

Preheat oven to 300° F (150° C).
In a bowl, combine flour, salt, baking powder
and baking soda. Mix well and set aside.
In another bowl, blend the brown and white
sugar with an electric mixer at medium speed.
Add the butter and whisk to form a grainy
paste. Gradually drop eggs into raised butter,
then add the walnuts, coffee powder, cocoa
powder and chocolate chips, and beat until well
blended. Add the flour mixture and knead until
smooth. Place 1 tbsp of the dough on the
buttered cookie sheet or non-stick baking tray,
keeping each mound 2 in (5 cm) apart from the
next. Before baking, flatten each mound until it
is about ½-in (1-cm) thick. Bake for 20 to 30
minutes, or until firm. Transfer the cookies onto
wire racks to cool before serving

Makes 4 dozen

◁ Carmen's Butter Crescents

8⅛ oz (227 g) unsalted butter • 1¼ cup (150 g/5¼ oz) icing sugar • ¼ tsp salt
¼ tsp baking soda • ½ cup (70 g/2½ oz) roasted cashew nuts, chopped
3¾ cups (450 g/16 oz) all-purpose flour, sieved

Preheat the oven to 300° F (150° C). In a bowl, work the butter, sugar,
salt, baking soda and cashew nuts with your hands until all the ingredients
are well mixed. Slowly incorporate the flour and continue to mix and knead
until all the ingredients are evenly blended. Roll a 1-oz (25-g) ball of cookie
dough between your palms to form a 3½-in (7-cm) log. Taper both ends
of the cylinder to create a crescent. Repeat this process until all the
dough is used up. Bake the crescents on a buttered cookie sheet or non-
stick baking tray for 20 to 30 minutes or until golden brown. Serve warm.

Makes 4 dozen

▽ Lychee Blend

(Lin Chii Pan)

4 whole lychees, halved
1 cup (100 g/3½ oz) crushed ice
⅜ cup (90 ml/3 fl oz) lychee juice
½ tbsp Thai sugar syrup (see Basics)

Place the whole lychees, lychee juice, syrup
and crushed ice into a blender and blend to a
smooth purée. Pour into a glass and garnish
with a fresh orchid.

Serves 1

▽ Thai Tropical Fruit Blend

(Nam Pol La Mai Roum Pan)

1 cup (100 g/3½ oz) crushed ice • 2 pineapple rings
2 large sections of papaya • 2 rambutans, halved
¼ cup (60 ml/2 oz) rambutan juice
⅛ cup (30 ml/1 fl oz) pineapple juice
⅛ cup (30 ml/1 fl oz) Thai sugar syrup (see Basics)
3 tsp lime juice

Place all the ingredients in a blender and blend
to a smooth purée. Garnish with a fresh orchid.

Serves 1

▽ Thompson Mai Thai

¼ cup (45 ml/1½ fl oz) white rum
⅛ cup (30 ml/1 fl oz) orange juice
⅛ cup (30 ml/1 fl oz) pineapple juice
⅛ cup (30 ml/1 fl oz) Thai sugar syrup (see Basics)
3 tsp grenadine • 3 tsp dark rum
1 pineapple spear • 1 maraschino cherry

Fill a cocktail shaker ¾ full with ice. Add the white rum, orange juice, pineapple juice, syrup and grenadine. Shake well, then strain into a glass. Float dark rum on top. Garnish with pineapple, cherry and a fresh orchid.

Serves 1

▽ Mango & Lime Juice Blend

(Nam Ma Muang Ma Nao)

2 cups (500 ml/1 pt 1 fl oz) water
1 large ripe mango, grated
½ cup (100 g/3½ oz) sugar
½ cup (130 ml/4⅓ fl oz) fresh carrot juice
pinch of salt • 1½ tbsp lime juice
1 cup (100 g/3½ oz) crushed ice

Boil water in a saucepan. Reduce heat to medium-high and add mangoes and sugar. Stir until sugar is dissolved and mangoes liquefied. Reduce to low heat and simmer for 5 minutes, stirring frequently. Remove and let cool. Blend with carrot juice, salt, lime juice and crushed ice to a smooth paste.

Serves 1

Appendices

Pastes and stocks are an essential part of Thai cooking, forming the base for curries, noodle and rice dishes. Sauces add flavor and piquancy, exciting and teasing the palate while complementing the food which they accompany.

▽ Plum Sauce (Nahm Jim Boui)

3 cups (750 ml/1 pt 9½ fl oz) water
1½ cups (300 g/10½ oz) sugar
½ tbsp salt • ¾ cup (180 ml/6 fl oz) vinegar
2 salted plums, deseeded • 1 tbsp salted plum juice

Boil water in a saucepan and add sugar, salt and vinegar. Stirring constantly, reduce heat and simmer for 10 minutes or until thickened. Add salted plums and plum juice. Mash the plums with a spoon and cook for 2 minutes.

Makes 1 cup (250 ml/8½ fl oz)

▽ Chilies in Fish Sauce
(Nahm Pla Prik)

12 to 14 bird's eye chilies, chopped • 4 garlic cloves, sliced thinly
10 tbsp fish sauce • 2 tbsp lime juice

Combine all the ingredients in a bowl and mix well to serve.

Makes 1 cup (250 ml/8½ fl oz)

▽ Northeastern Thai Sauce (Nahm Jim Jeow)

2 tsp lime juice • 6 tsp fish sauce • 4 tbsp tamarind juice
¼ tsp chili powder • 1 tsp white sugar • 4 shallots, sliced thinly
¼ tsp roasted rice (see Basics) • 1 tsp chopped spring onion

Combine all the ingredients in a bowl and mix well to serve.

Makes 1 cup (250 ml/8½ fl oz)

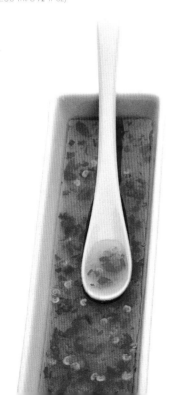

Mussaman Curry Paste

(Nahm Prik Gang Mussaman)

½ tsp coriander seeds, roasted and ground
2 tsp cloves, roasted and ground
2 tsp cinnamon, roasted and ground
2 tsp nutmeg, roasted and ground
2 tsp fennel, roasted and ground
½ tsp peppercorns, roasted and ground
1 tbsp roasted cardamom seeds, ground
36 long dried red chilies, deseeded, soaked and drained • 5 coriander roots
4 tbsp lemon grass, chopped
2 tbsp galangal, chopped
5 tbsp garlic, chopped
7 tbsp red shallots, chopped
4 bay leaves • ½ cup (125 ml/4¼ fl oz) oil

Place all the dry spices in a wok and roast gently. Let cool and grind to a fine powder. Add oil to a hot wok and roast chilies, coriander roots, lemon grass, galangal, garlic and red shallots until fragrant. With a blender, purée the roasted herbs and work in oil, spices and bay leaves until smooth. (Note: This paste is best used when fresh, but it can be stored in an airtight container in the refrigerator for up to 2 weeks or in the freezer for up to 2 months.)

Makes 2 cups (450 g/1 lb)

Panaeng Curry Paste

(Nahm Prik Gang Panaeng)

12 long red dried chilies
½ tsp peppercorns, roasted
1 tsp coriander seeds, roasted

½ tsp cumin seeds, roasted • ½ tsp salt
4 slices galangal, chopped
¼ tsp kaffir lime rind
2 stalks lemon grass, chopped
5 tbsp shallots, chopped
5 tbsp garlic cloves, chopped • 4 tbsp oil
½ cup (75 g/2⅝ oz) raw peanuts

Place all the spices in a wok and roast gently. Let cool and then grind to a fine powder. Add the oil to a hot wok and stir-fry the galangal, kaffir lime, lemon grass, shallots, and garlic cloves and until fragrant. Using a blender, purée the roasted herbs and slowly work in the remaining oil, spices and peanuts until a smooth paste is achieved. (Note: This paste is best used when fresh, but it can be stored in an airtight container in the refrigerator for 2 weeks or in the freezer for up to 2 months.)

Makes 2 cups (450 g/1 lb)

Red Curry Paste

(Nahm Prik Gaeng Daeng)

13 small dried chilies
1 tbsp coriander seeds • 1 tsp cumin seeds
2 tbsp shallots, chopped
4 tbsp garlic, chopped
1 tbsp galangal, chopped
2 tbsp lemon grass, chopped
2 tsp kaffir lime rind, chopped
1 tbsp coriander root, chopped
20 peppercorns • 1 tsp shrimp paste

Soak dried chilies in hot water for 15 minutes and remove seeds. In a wok over low heat, dry-fry the coriander and cumin seeds for about 5 minutes, then grind into a powder. Place the rest of the ingredients except the shrimp paste into a blender and blend well. Add the

coriander-cumin seed mixture and shrimp paste, and blend until smooth. (Note: This paste is best used when fresh, but it can be stored in an airtight container in the refrigerator for 2 weeks or in the freezer for up to 2 months.)

Makes 2 cups (450 g/1 lb)

Green Curry Paste (Nahm Prik Gaeng Giow Warn)

5 tbsp shallots, chopped
5 tbsp garlic cloves, chopped
½ tsp kaffir lime rind, chopped
2 stalks lemon grass, chopped
4 slices galangal, chopped
¼ tsp peppercorns
10 green bird's eye chilies, chopped
20 red bird's eye chilies, chopped
3 coriander roots, scraped and chopped
1 tsp shrimp paste

Using a food processor, purée all ingredients into a smooth paste. (Note: This paste is best used when fresh, but it can be stored in an airtight container in the refrigerator for 2 weeks or in the freezer for up to 2 months.)

Makes 2 cups (450 g/1 lb)

Roasted Chili Paste (Nahm Prik Phao)

Oil for frying • 3 tbsp garlic, chopped
3 tbsp shallots, chopped
3 tbsp dried red chilies, coarsely chopped
1 tbsp shrimp paste • 1 tbsp fish sauce
2 tsp sugar

Fry the garlic and shallots in the oil until golden. Remove them from the oil and set aside. Do the same for the chilies. Using a pestle and mortar, pound the shrimp paste together with the fried chilies, garlic and shallots, forming a smooth paste. Stir-fry the paste in a little oil, and season with the fish sauce and sugar. (Note: This paste is best used fresh but can be refrigerated in an airtight container for up to 1 month.)

Makes 1 cup (225 g/8 oz)

Steamed Glutinous Rice
(Khao Niao Neung)

2½ cups (500g/1 lb 5½ oz) uncooked glutinous rice
2 cups (500 ml/1 pt 1 fl oz) water

Wash the rice and soak in water. Drain the rice and place on a steamer tray lined with a cheesecloth or banana leaf. Cover and steam for 25 to 30 minutes until cooked. Keep covered until needed.

Serves 4

Curry Powder
(Pong Ka Ree)

1 tbsp black peppercorns
3 tbsp coriander seeds
3 tbsp cumin seeds • 1 clove
1 tbsp fennel seeds
20 Thai cardamom pods
15 long dried red chilies
3 tbsp chilli powder • 5 tbsp ground ginger
7 tbsp turmeric

In a medium-hot wok, dry-fry the peppercorns, coriander seeds, cumin seeds, clove, fennel seds and cardamom for 2 minutes. Using a mortar and pestle, grind spices to a fine powder. Add dried chilies, chili powder, ginger and turmeric and pound until fine, then pass through a fine sieve.

Makes ½ cup (30 g/1 oz)

Deep-Fried Minced Garlic
(Kra-tiam Sap Jiaw)

20 medium cloves garlic
large pinch of salt • 4 tbsp oil

Mince the garlic with the salt. Stir-fry in oil over medium-high heat, stirring until golden brown. Remove garlic from oil and allow oil to cool. Combine garlic and oil, and store in an airtight container.

Makes 5 cups (850 g/1 lb 14 oz)

Ground Roasted Rice (Khao Krua)

1 cup (180 g/6⅜ oz) uncooked glutinous rice • 2 slices galangal • 3 kaffir lime leaves

Dry-fry the rice over low heat in a wok. Add galangal and kaffir lime leaves, toasting the rice until golden brown. Remove the galangal and leaves, and let cool. Grind into medium to fine powder.

Makes 1 cup (55 g/2 oz)

Chicken Stock
(Sup Gai)

2 lbs (910 g) chicken bones
6⅓ cups (1.5 L/3 pt 2¾ fl oz) water
pinch of black pepper
3 long stalks Chinese celery
½ white turnip, untrimmed
7 cloves garlic, bruised

Place all the ingredients in a pot and cover with water. Bring to a boil and simmer for 45 minutes. Strain to use.

Makes 3 cups (750 ml/1 pt 5½ fl oz)

Thai Sugar Syrup (Nahm Cheum)

4 cups (800 g/1 lb 12 oz) white sugar
4 cups (1 L/1 pt 14 fl oz) water
2 pandanus leaves, knotted

Place sugar, water and pandanus leaves in a pot and simmer until sugar has dissolved. Remove leaves, strain mixture and cool.

Makes 2 cups (500 ml/17 fl oz)

Perfumed Water (Nahm Loy Dok Mali)

7 cups (1 L 680 ml/2 pt 17 fl oz) water
18 jasmine blossoms

Combine the jasmines with the water, cover and leave to stand overnight. Strain before using.

Makes 7 cups (1 L 680 ml/2 pt 17 fl oz)

Asian kale (phak kaa-naa)

The flavor and texture of its stems are largely similar to Western broccoli. It lacks large flower heads, and instead bears large dark green leaves and small white flowers. Also known both as Asian kale and Chinese broccoli, this is very popular as a vegetable dish.

basil leaves, Thai (bai horapha)

Bearing medium to large leaves, Thai basil has a distinctively sweet anise flavor. It is used to spice up stir-fried dishes, curries, salads, and also as a garnish for soups.

betel leaves (bai cha-phluu)

These are thick and dark green in color, and pointed at one end. Hot and peppery in taste, they are wrapped around various fragrant spices, and are chewed after meals to aid digestion. Also thought to provide relief from coughs and congestion of the chest.

cardamom pods, Thai (loog gra waan)

The Thai cardamom has a white pod, as compared to the more common green pods that are mainly grown in India and Sri Lanka. Both taste similar. Typically added to rice dishes, curries and also sweets.

chilies (prik)

Bird's eye chilies (prik khii nuu) are the smallest and hottest variety of Thai chili. Both red and green varities are used in curries and relishes. Long chilies (prik chii faa) are longer and milder, but richer in flavor. Commonly used in stir-fries, salads and curry pastes.

chili sauce (sauce sriracha)

This full-bodied, spicy orange-colored sauce is served with deep-fried dishes.

Chinese cabbage, pickled

Also referred to as celery cabbage, with pale green leaves and white stems. Most commonly encountered in cabbage rolls and kim chi.

Chinese celery (kuen chaii)

This Asian variety is entirely different from the Western variety. It has relatively limp, slender stems with particularly aromatic leaves, and is used more as a herb rather than a vegetable. Commonly used to garnish soups, rice dishes and stir-fried dishes.

Chinese chives

More flavorsome than the Western variety, these garlic chives are thicker and flatter, and typically bear long, dark green leaves. The flowerbud is also edible. They are used as a herb and make a good vegetable dish as well.

Chinese five-spice powder (kruang yaa chene)

Opinions vary about the ingredients that go into this traditional Chinese spice blend, but the essential basics comprise Szechuan pepper, star anise, cinnamon, fennel and cloves. Some varieties also include ground ginger and licorice root.

Chinese mustard cabbage (canton)

A highly versatile vegetable, with a slight mustard flavor that gains intensity as the plant matures. Can be used for salads, stir-fried and baked dishes, and also soups. Sometimes also known as gai choy or Oriental mustard.

Chinese yam

Also known as the air potato, this is an edible tuber that is used both for cooking as well as in traditional Chinese medicine. Among other benefits, it aids lung and kidney functions. It is starchier than other yam varieties, with a longer and more slender appearance.

coconut (ma praow)

To make coconut cream (hua gati) and coconut milk (hang gati), blend the flesh of 1 coconut in a food processor with a little water until smooth. Strain through a muslin cloth into a bowl and allow to separate for 30 minutes. Skim the cream from the top, leaving the milk in the bowl.

coriander leaves (phak chii)

Also referred to as Chinese parsley, this strongly aromatic herb is used to garnish soups and salads, and flavor cooked dishes. Thai cuisine in fact utilises the entire coriander plant for various preparations, from its leaves and stems, right down to the roots.

coriander root (raak phak chii)

The root of the Chinese coriander plant, often pounded and added to spicy pastes or marinades.

cumin, ground (med yii raa)

Ground cumin is an important ingredient in practically every sort of curry paste and spice mix. In raw form, these are tiny, aromatic seeds with an earthy flavor. Black cumin is considered relatively sweeter than common cumin.

durian (turian)

Indigenous to parts of Southeast Asia, this tropical fruit has a thick skin covered with hard spikes, and gives off a pungent odor. The flesh within is dense and creamy, and comes in various shades of custard. Known regionally as the "King of Fruits", and believed to possess aphrodisiac properties.

fettuccine

Long and flat pasta noodles, very common in Italian cuisine.

fish maw, dried (khra phor pla)

The dried stomach lining that has been removed from a large fish, cleaned, dried and finally fried. When used in cooking, this has to be first soaked in water for a few hours, sliced, and then typically boiled. Although it has close to no distinctive taste, it adds a chewy texture to dishes, and very quickly absorbs the dominant flavors.

fish sauce (nahm pla)

Often used in place of salt, this is a salty light-brown liquid made from extracts of fermented anchovies or salted shrimp. With its signature pungent flavor, this is a very popular condiment at Thai dining tables, although the flavor deteriorates once it has been exposed to air. Also known as fish soy or fish gravy.

galangal (kha)

This pinkish tuber has larger roots than the common ginger, and adds a slightly peppery flavor to curry pastes in Thai cooking. Believed to help respiratory infections and aid digestion. Also known as Siamese ginger, and goes particularly well with seafood.

garlic (kra-tiam)

Thai garlic is generally small but with a very distinctive flavour. Deep-fried garlic is typically used as a garnish in many Thai dishes.

garlic, pickled (kra-tiam dong)

Pickled with vinegar, sugar and salt, it is commonly used in salads or as a condiment. Available in most Asian grocery stores.

ginger (khing)

Used in many Thai salads, soups and curries, fresh young ginger should be firm and juicy with a smooth, pinkish-beige skin.

green mango (ma muang dib)

Hard and green when mature. There are a few varieties of Thai origin, all relatively elongated in shape and with varying degrees of sourness. Often used sliced in salads, pickled, soaked in vinegar or fish sauce, or eaten plain.

green papaya (malagaw dib)

When still unripe, this fruit has dark green skin and pale flesh. In Thailand, it is most commonly peeled, shredded and mixed with garlic, chilies and other ingredients to make spicy salads. It also contains the enzyme papain, which has a tenderizing effect on meat.

jackfruit (kha-nun)
Once removed from the seeds, the dark yellow flesh of this fruit is typically added to a fruit salad or dessert. The unripe fruit is also cooked and eaten as a vegetable dish.

jasmine blossom (ma-li)
Flowers of the jasmine plant are used to add a pleasant fragrance to drinking water, tea and desserts. Best picked around evening time.

kaffir lime (makrut)
Although this green citrus fruit bears little juice, it is used to give tartness to Thai dishes. Its leaves and peel are added to gravies and curry pastes. Can be substituted with regular lime.

lemon grass (ta krai)
Also known in the Southeast Asian region as *serai*. The lower stalk is highly aromatic, and is a key ingredient in signature Thai dishes, including spicy *dtom yam* soups.

limes (ma-nao)
Limes and lime juice are used extensively in Thai cooking as a souring agent. Thai limes are smaller and slightly sweeter than regular limes.

lychee (lin chii)
Approximately the size of a large lime, the white flesh of this juicy, succulent fruit comes encased in a reddish, leathery skin, and has a black stone in the center. Thie fruit is available all year round, and is typically used in tropical fruit salads.

mangoes (ma-muang)
Sticky rice (*khao niao*) with ripe mangoes is one of the best-known Thai desserts. Unripe green mangoes are used in curries, relishes and salads, or eaten raw with sweet fish sauce (*nahm pla warn*).

mint (sa-ra-nae)
Mint is used in many northern Thai salads and as a garnish in soup and noodle dishes.

morning glory (pak bung)
In its raw form, this vegetable is an important ingredient in papaya salads, which are a favorite throughout Thailand. It can also be stir-fried or added to curries. Otherwise known as water spinach, the Thai version has broader leaves and thicker stems than the more common Chinese variety. Both are similar in flavor.

mushrooms (het)
Straw mushrooms (*het faang*) are the most common of all Thai mushrooms and are used in salads, soups and curries. Oyster mushrooms can be substituted for straw mushrooms. Fresh and fried shiitake mushrooms (*het horm*) are used to add flavor to soups and fried dishes.

noodles, broad rice (kuay tiew)
Rice noodles that are broader in width and slightly similar in appearance to fettuccine. Typically stir-fried, or served in soups and sauces. Also known as rice ribbon noodles.

noodles, thin rice (sen lek)
Rice noodles cut in thread-like strands.

oyster sauce (nahm man hoii)
A thick, dark sauce used extensively in Chinese cuisine; unlike soy sauce, this is used as a seasoning, but not as a condiment.

palm sugar (nahm taan piip)
A soft caramel-flavored sugar, made from the sap of either the coconut or palm tree. When used in solid form, this needs to be grated or scraped into slivers with a knife before use. Depending on the recipe, brown sugar is sometimes accepted as a substitute.

pandanus leaves (bai toey)
Also known as screwpine leaves, these are used to flavor desserts and wrap food, as well as to impart a natural green coloring to dishes.

peppercorns, black and white (prik thai)
Peppercorns are berries that grow on the pepper plant. Different stages of maturity result in three types of peppercorns: black, white and green. Black peppercorn is the most pungent while white peppercorn has a milder flavor. The latter also blends well into clear dishes.

peppercorns, Thai green (prik thai)
These under-ripe berries are more subtle in flavor as compared to the black and white varieties, but are nevertheless very popular in Thai cooking.

pomelo (som oo)
Probably the largest fruit in the citrus family, this generally looks like a large grapefruit, and has a thick skin that is either green or yellow. The pulp ranges from yellow to pink in color, and on the whole is sweeter but less juicy than the grapefruit. Also sometimes known as Chinese grapefruit or Bali lemon.

rambutans (ngaw)
This fruit's juicy, translucent flesh clings to a stone, and is found inside a red, leathery skin covered with coarse hair-like filaments. Served in fruit salads, as a dessert topping, or frozen in jellies. Largely grown in Malaysia.

rice, glutinous (khao niao)
Naturally sticky rice, eaten as a staple at meals, and also used in puddings and food stuffings.

rice, jasmine (khao)
Also commonly known as Thai fragrant rice, it is available in both white and brown varieties, and earns its name from the light jasmine fragrance that is given off as the rice cooks. Its delicious aroma makes it a very popular staple in Thai cooking.

red shallots (horm daeng)
Used in curry pastes, soups and salads, these small red shallots can be sliced and deep-fried (*horm jiaw*) to use as a garnish, or roasted (*horm pao*) to add a smoky flavor to soups.

shiitake mushroom, dried (het horm)
After drying, the flavor of these mushrooms naturally deepens as compared to when fresh. These need to be soaked in water before use, and the water can later be reused as a broth.

shrimp paste (ga-pi)
This dried paste is available in various forms, from cans and jars to small bricks wrapped in paper or plastic. Often roasted before use to bring out its aromatic flavor. Available at most Asian grocery stores, and sometimes referred to as *belacan*, its Malay name.

tamarind juice (ma khaam piak)
The sour pulp from the pod of the tamarind tree is used to add a sour tinge to soups and sauces. Fresh or preserved tamarind is soaked and mashed in hot water, which is then strained and used for cooking. Different sources tend to be of varying degrees of sourness, and there are sweet varieties too. Commonly known in Asia as *assam*.

tapioca pearls (saku)
Balls of chewy tapioca starch, approximately the size of playing marbles.

vermicelli, dried bean (woon sen)
Translucent noodles made from mung beans, also referred to as cellophane noodles and glass noodles. These hard strands should be soaked in warm water before using, then cut and boiled or added to stir-fried dishes.

wolfberries
Dried and sold in packets, these seasonal reddish-orange berries are known for adding a pleasantly sweet flavor to cooked dishes. They are believed to be good for the eyes due to their very high carotene content. Also referred to as boxthorn.

Directory | Acknowledgments

Saladaeng Café
120/1 Saladaeng Soi 1,
Silom Road, Bangkok, Thailand
Tel: (662) 266 9167

Thompson
Jim Thompson House Museum
6 Soi Kasemsan 2,
Rama 1 Road, Bangkok, Thailand
Tel: (662) 216 7368

Cafe ♂'
9 Surawong Road, Bangkok, Thailand
Tel: (662) 632 8100

mythai
LG7 Lower Ground Floor
Star Hill Shopping Centre
181 Jalan Bukit Bintang,
Kuala Lumpur, Malaysia
Tel: (603) 2148 6151

FROM LEFT: Thompson Bar and Restaurant is a strikingly modern affair within the compound of the Jim Thompson House; mythai in Kuala Lumpur is an oasis of calm in the heart of prime shopping district Bukit Bintang; the interior of Saladaeng Café is a discreet, tasteful blend of Asian and Western décor.

PREVIOUS PAGES: An architect by profession, Jim Thompson supervised the design of his house, which is made up of an assembly of traditional Thai structures.

I wish to express my sincere appreciation to all of the talented cooks, bakers, wait staff and office staff of the Jim Thompson Thai Silk Company for making this cookbook possible and whose dedication and hard work continue to make our company a success.

Patrick Booth